HOME REPAIR AND IMPROVEMENT

ULTIMATE DECKS

OTHER PUBLICATIONS:

DO IT YOURSELF
Total Golf
How to Fix It
The Time-Life Complete Gardener
The Art of Woodworking

COOKING
Weight Watchers® Smart Choice Recipe Collection
Great Taste/Low Fat
Williams-Sonoma Kitchen Library

HISTORY
Our American Century
What Life was Like
The American Story
Voices of the Civil War
The American Indians
Lost Civilizations
Mysteries of the Unknown
Time Frame
The Civil War
Cultural Atlas

TIME-LIFE KIDS
Student Library
Library of First Questions and Answers
A Child's First Library of Learning
I Love Math
Nature Company Discoveries
Understanding Science & Nature

SCIENCE/NATURE
Voyage Through the Universe

For information on and a full description
of any of the Time-Life Books series listed above,
please call 1-800-621-7026 or write:

Reader Information
Time-Life Customer Service
P.O. Box C-32068
Richmond Virginia 23261-2068

HOME REPAIR AND IMPROVEMENT

ULTIMATE DECKS

BY THE EDITORS OF TIME-LIFE BOOKS, ALEXANDRIA, VIRGINIA

The Consultants

Richard Day has built three homes for himself and his family, the most recent with a wraparound redwood deck. Mr. Day spent eight years with the Portland Cement Association as a writer and editor, and has written numerous articles on home improvement for *Popular Science*. Based in California, he has written two books about building decks and in 1992 his most recent decks book won first prize in the National Association of Home and Workshop Writers/Stanley Tools Do-It-Yourself Writing Contest.

Michael Tustin has formal training in architectural drafting and commercial construction, and has been working in the home improvement and decking industry for 25 years. He is owner of M.R.T. Home Improvement, and in 1987 he founded Supreme Sundeck Industries, specializing in custom-built decks for the Montreal area.

CONTENTS

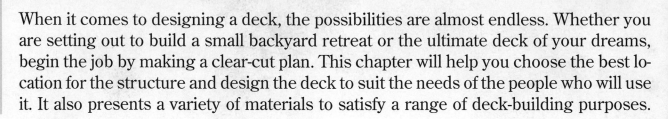

1

Plans and Preliminaries

When it comes to designing a deck, the possibilities are almost endless. Whether you are setting out to build a small backyard retreat or the ultimate deck of your dreams, begin the job by making a clear-cut plan. This chapter will help you choose the best location for the structure and design the deck to suit the needs of the people who will use it. It also presents a variety of materials to satisfy a range of deck-building purposes.

Even the most beautiful deck may go largely unused if it is constantly baked by the sun or has an unattractive setting. These and other problems can often be avoided if you select an appropriate location before you begin planning.

Mapping Your Lot: To choose a good spot for a deck, you need to find out what factors may influence its use. The first step in this process is to draw up a site plan *(opposite)*—a sketch of your lot that includes such features as sun and shade, wind direction, and views; as well as other considerations like changes in lot level and locations of downspouts. In some cases, you may be able to obtain the original architect's site plan or deed maps from your municipal government, the mortgage company, or the property's previous owner. Otherwise, you'll have to take measurements and draw up the plan yourself.

Legal Restrictions: A number of regulations affect the placement of a deck. Zoning ordinances stipulate what percentage of your lot can be covered by structures. They also specify how far the deck must be set back from the property lines. Architectural review boards in certain neighborhoods or requirements in the house deed itself may put additional restrictions on the location.

Sketching in the Deck: Once you've completed the site plan, choose a spot, taking into consideration the factors listed in the box below. Then, roughly sketch in the shape and size of the deck on the site plan. Once you are satisfied with the location, you are ready to begin designing the deck itself.

Choosing a Deck Location

✔ Will the deck violate zoning restrictions, setback laws, or lot-coverage requirements?

✔ Will the deck be accessible from the desired room of the house, or can you add a door there if necessary?

✔ Will you need to move trees or large shrubs to make room for the proposed deck?

✔ Will water from gutters and downspouts drain onto the deck or undermine posts, or can you divert it to another area?

✔ Will the deck block light to rooms underneath it?

✔ How much sun does the spot receive, and during what parts of the day? Will an overhead provide enough shade for a too-sunny deck?

✔ Is the location private, or can you shield the deck with screens?

✔ Is the site excessively windy, or can screens or plantings serve as windbreaks?

✔ Will the location offer attractive views from the deck?

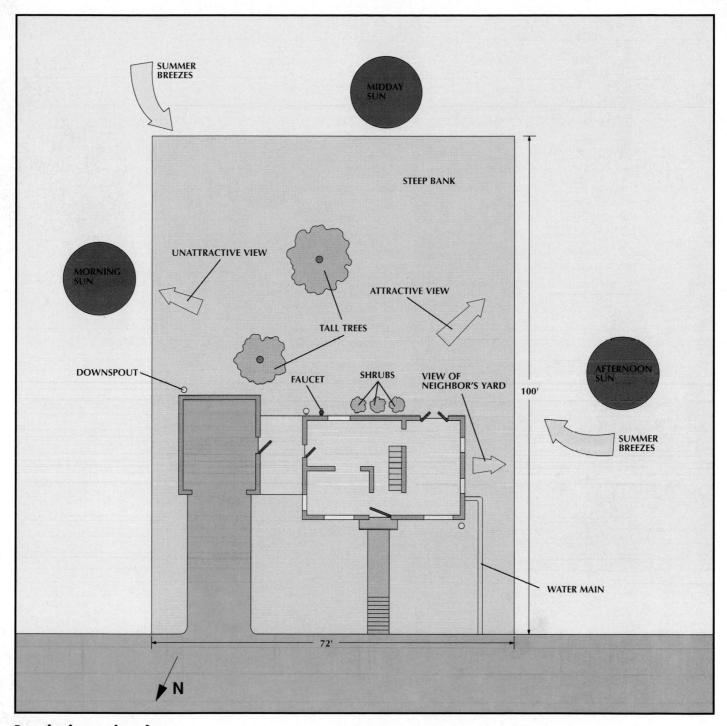

Developing a site plan.

◆ On a sheet of graph paper, draw a map of your lot to scale and mark the dimensions. Then add a floor plan of the house's ground floor.

◆ Draw in downspouts, outdoor faucets, and underground utilities.

◆ Indicate attractive and unattractive views, as well as views into neighboring yards.

◆ Note level changes and steep banks.

◆ Indicate existing trees, shrubs, and plantings.

◆ Show the sun's morning, midday, and afternoon positions, as well as the direction of summer breezes.

Once you've settled on a location for the deck, you can experiment with designs. On the next pages are illustrations that suggest some of the possibilities. From the starting point of a simple rectangle *(pages 20-41)*, you can make minor modifications to add interest or solve a certain construction problem. Some of these changes include cutting off a corner or wrapping the deck around two sides of the house *(pages 42-51)*. You can also vary the height of the deck, adding one or more levels to define areas of activity or highlight special features *(pages 52-59)*.

Planning the Deck: When you have decided on a design for the deck, review the framing methods presented in Chapter 2 to find the ones that are appropriate for your design. Choose among these examples and combine those that will best create the shape and style you want. You can also begin thinking about the details that influence its final appearance, such as the decking pattern and the stair and railing styles *(Chapter 3)*; as well as the accessories such as benches, planters, screens, and overheads *(Chapter 4)*.

TRANSFORMING AN ORDINARY DECK

A simple deck.
The design shown above is one of the easiest designs to build: It is a simple rectangle attached to the house, with a set of stairs added at a right angle. While this deck is perfectly functional, it has few interesting features to give it charm and character.

Easy improvements.

The deck above has the same basic shape as the rectangular one opposite, but slight modifications make it more appealing. One corner is cut off at an angle *(pages 42-44)* and the stairs exit that corner. A platform *(pages 52-53)*—also with cut-off corners—serves as a landing in front of the door to the house and interrupts the flat expanse of the deck surface.

A GALLERY OF LAYOUTS

A hillside deck.

Sloping ground is no deterrent to building an attractive deck. Where the yard rises sharply along the house, a two-level deck such as the one at left can mirror the terrain. More levels can be added to cover a very hilly lot. To build a multi-level deck, construct the upper level first, then attach the lower ones sequentially *(pages 54-55).*

A WOODED RETREAT

The deck in this photograph is built on rocky terrain that slopes away from the house. To adapt to the changes in ground height, the deck was built in two levels with broad steps between them. The lower section extends beyond the side of the house to keep open the view of the woods from the glass doors. A set of steps links the lower deck to a wooded pathway, and built-in benches provide permanent seating under the canopy of trees.

A wraparound design.
A deck that wraps around the corner of a house such as the one at left can extend the deck and create a cozy area sheltered by the house. Such a deck requires only minor changes in the basic rectangular design *(pages 45-48)* and the standard decking pattern *(page 66)*.

A low-level deck.

In some cases you may want to build a deck directly on the ground *(page 33)*. In the example above, the lower-level framing incorporates an opening *(pages 49-51)* for a garden pool. An upper level, which rests directly on the lower one *(pages 52-53)*, is situated away from traffic passing through the door, creating an ideal space for activities such as dining.

A freestanding deck.

A freestanding deck *(page 40)* is framed slightly differently from one that is attached to a house. You can build such a deck next to the house, or set it in a corner of the yard to serve as a quiet retreat away from activity. The example at right has a cut-off corner *(pages 42-44)*, a broad step *(pages 56-57)*, and an overhead *(pages 112-115)*.

A second-story deck.

A high deck is built in much the same way as one at a low level, but the posts must be braced to make it strong and stable. If you want to access the yard, you must add a long staircase. In the de- sign above, the stairs change direction halfway down to prevent them from extending too far out into the yard. If you are considering building a second-story deck, keep in mind that it will create heavy shade on any windows underneath it.

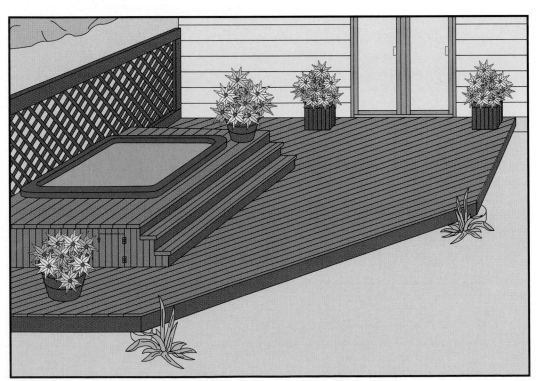

A deck with a hot tub.

An opening can be framed in a deck to accommodate a hot tub *(pages 58-59)*. In this example, the tub is set on a higher level that has a skirt around it to hide the the base of the tub. A screen is placed behind the tub for privacy and to shield bathers from wind.

Details such as the decking pattern and stair and railing construction have a great influence on the style of a deck. Straight decking is the simplest to install, but you can dress up a deck with a variety of other patterns. You can also incorporate accessories such as benches, planters, screens, and overheads.

In designing these details, choose elements that will harmonize with the house and blend well with each other.

For example, stair treads and bench seats of 2-by-2s with picture-frame trim *(pages 79-80)* make a good match, but avoid combining too many elements. If you choose an elaborate decking pattern, keep benches and railings simple. Information on these details is presented in Chapters 3 and 4. Following the basic building methods shown there, you can adapt any of the styles to create your own.

A DECK THAT MATCHES THE HOUSE

Carefully chosen details can make a deck look like an integral part of the house. The dark oak stain on the deck in the photograph blends with the Tudor-style trim of the house, and the slope of the overhead echoes the house roof. To emphasize the country-cottage look, the railings feature a heart-shaped motif. Railing posts are topped with decorative finials.

Not only do the materials you choose for your deck establish its appearance, they also, to a large extent, determine the life span of the structure.

The Understructure: The posts, beams, and joists of a deck should be made of lumber that has been pressure-treated with a preservative and an insecticide—typically chromated copper arsenate (CCA)—to withstand rot and insects. The woods most commonly available with this preparation are southern pine and Douglas-fir. Pick lumber that is rated No. 2 or better. Consult the dealer to find out whether you need to brush preservative onto cut ends and drilled holes to maintain the warranty.

Decking, Stairs, and Railings: For these highly visible parts of the deck,

pressure-treated lumber is the most economical choice; however, some people prefer the appearance of the more expensive redwood or cedar. Grades of cedar and redwood that are composed of all heartwood—the darker wood from the center of the tree—are naturally resistant to rot and insects. Lower grades require a protective finish *(pages 96-97)*.

Decking boards are typically 2-by-4s or 2-by-6s; for a less massive look, you can buy special 5/4 decking with rounded edges, referred to as "radius-edge decking." Nonwood products are also available *(below)*.

Hardware and Fasteners: All deck hardware and fasteners—framing anchors, nails, screws, and bolts—must be weather resistant. Galvanized fasteners are the most common choice, but deck screws

with an additional resin coating last even longer.

Concrete: To build post footings and slabs at the bottom of stairs and ramps, it is simplest to buy sacks of premixed concrete: dry ingredients to which you add only water. About $2\frac{1}{2}$ cubic feet—enough for one shallow footing—can be mixed by hand in a wheelbarrow *(opposite)*. If the footings are deep, you can rent an electric mixer that can handle up to 6 cubic feet. For a large project with many deep footings, consider having the concrete delivered by a ready-mix truck.

⚠️ **CAUTION** *Pressure-treated wood contains toxic chemicals. Always wash your hands thoroughly after handling it, and do not burn it.*

ALTERNATIVES TO WOOD

Deck boards of solid vinyl or wood/plastic composites will not warp, crack, or rot, and are virtually maintenance-free. Vinyl deck boards *(right)* are available in a range of solid colors and snap into place on metal rails fastened to the deck framing. Wood composite decking resembles real wood and is fastened with nails or screws like ordinary lumber. Railing systems of either material can generally be purchased with the deck boards.

TOOLS
Wheelbarrow
Bucket
Mason's hoe
Square shovel

 **MATERIALS**
Premixed concrete

 **SAFETY TIPS**
Wet or dry, concrete is caustic—wear gloves, goggles, and a dust mask when mixing it.

MIXING CONCRETE BY HAND

1. Mixing in the water.
◆ Empty the premixed dry concrete ingredients into a wheelbarrow and, with a mason's hoe, create a hollow in the middle of the material.
◆ Slowly pour about three-quarters of the required quantity of water into the depression *(right)*.
◆ Push the dry ingredients into the water, mixing until all the water has been absorbed. Then, turn the concrete over two or three times with the hoe.
◆ Add water a little at a time until the mixture completely coats all the coarse aggregate; leave any unused water in the bucket until you have adjusted the consistency *(Step 2)*.

2. Testing the consistency.
◆ Smooth the surface of the mixture with the back of a square shovel.
◆ Jab the edge of the shovel into the concrete to form grooves. If the surface is smooth and the grooves are distinct, the concrete is ready to use *(left)*. If the surface roughens or the grooves are indistinct, add a small amount of water. If the surface is wet or the grooves collapse, add a small amount of dry ingredients.
◆ Retest the batch until the consistency is correct. Then, note the quantity of dry ingredients and water used for subsequent batches.

Building the Understructure

Beneath its smooth decking and attractive railings, a deck is supported by a sturdy system of joists, beams, and posts. This understructure must be carefully laid out so that the finished deck is square and level, and engineered to carry the weight of the building materials as well as the furnishings and the people who use the deck.

The key to a solid and long-lasting deck is a well designed frame, or understructure. Carefully calculating the spacing and size of the framing members is an essential part of the planning process, and can help you save on materials and labor. Most decks are framed in a similar manner—a grid of posts supports beams, and the beams support a network of joists. As described below and opposite, a deck can be attached to a house or held up by posts on all sides.

Spans and Spacing: In planning a deck, you will need to determine the length and size of the framing members, and how far apart to space them. Make your calculations using the charts on page 22, which give figures for southern pine and Douglas-fir graded No. 2 or better—the two most economical lumber options.

Compute the information for the joists first, then proceed to the data for the beams and the posts. Keep in mind that the spacing between the beams equals the distance the joists can span from beam to beam, and that post spacing is the same as beam span. Since the size and the spacing of one element affects the size and the spacing of the others, you probably will need to work back and forth between the charts to determine the ideal arrangement. As you make your calculations, you may discover that more than one set of figures is appropriate—you usually have a choice between a smaller number of large structural members or a larger number of small ones.

Digging holes and casting concrete footings for the posts is generally the most time-consuming and costly part of the job, so it is best to minimize the number of posts and beams where possible. The final design will be determined not only by the allowable spans and spacings, but also by any special layout requirements of the deck shape and decking pattern *(pages 42-57 and 66-71).*

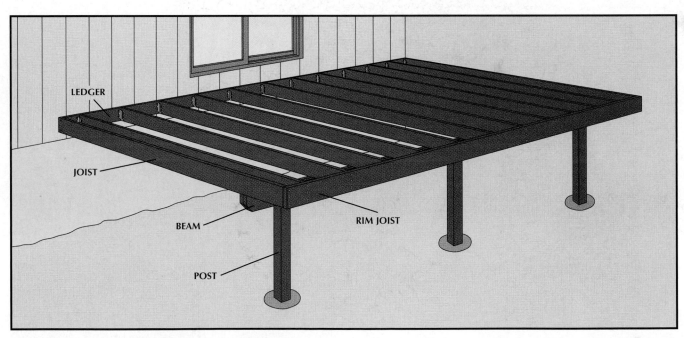

LEDGER

JOIST

BEAM

RIM JOIST

POST

Framing an attached deck.

On an attached deck, one side is held up by a ledger fastened to the house; the other side is supported by a beam sitting on a row of posts set in concrete footings. The joists hang from the ledger and rest on the beam, and a rim joist caps the ends of the joists. When the house has overlapping siding such as clapboard, a section of the siding is cut away to provide a flat surface on which to attach the ledger, and flashing is installed over the ledger to keep water from infiltrating the house wall.

In the framing design above, the beams are cantilevered—they project beyond the posts. The joists also project beyond the beams and posts. With this structure, the posts are recessed somewhat under the deck, so that slight inaccuracies in their positions will be hidden. In addition, cantilevering the joists and beams allows the distance from one support to the next to be reduced.

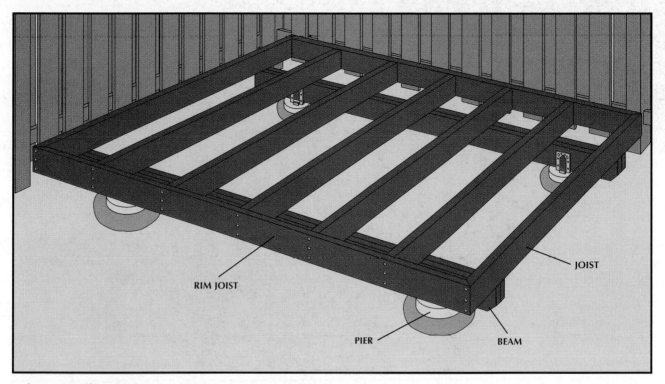

JOIST

RIM JOIST

PIER   BEAM

A freestanding deck.

This design is essentially the same as the one for an attached deck *(opposite)*, except that both sides of the frame are supported by beams. The example shown above is low to the ground, so the beams sit directly on concrete piers; a higher freestanding deck would be supported by posts.

While this design is intended for structures set away from the house—such as a deck in a corner of a yard—it is also practical for a deck next to a house that has overlapping siding, since the siding will not have to be cut away to accommodate the ledger of an attached deck.

A DECK WITH A FLUSH BEAM

An alternative to cantilevering joists is to place them on the same plane as the beam *(right)*. An advantage of this design is that the area underneath is more accessible for storage because there are no beams below the joists; but the design is also a good choice for a ground-level deck since it can be set lower than a deck with cantilevered joists. One drawback is that, to align correctly, the posts must be positioned more accurately than for a deck with cantilevered joists. The design illustrated at right is for an attached deck—a freestanding structure would have at least two flush beams.

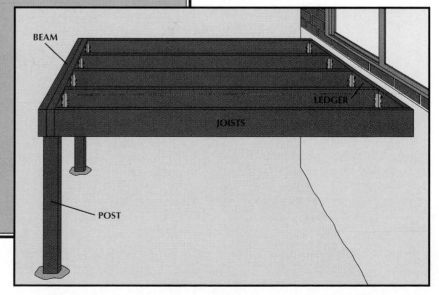

BEAM

LEDGER

JOISTS

POST

CALCULATING LUMBER SIZES AND SPACINGS

Determining joist size and spans.

The spacing of the joists is determined by the selection of decking lumber. Decking of 2-by-6s and 2-by-4s can span joists spaced 24 inches apart—or 16 inches if the decking is laid diagonally—while 5/4 decking must be supported by joists spaced every 16 inches—or 12 inches if laid diagonally. In the chart at right, the columns under the joist spacings indicate the joist span—which equals the beam spacing—for the different joist sizes. By increasing the size of the joist lumber, the span is increased, potentially cutting down on the number of beams and posts. For instance, if you plan to use diagonal 2-by-4 decking, the joist spacing is 16 inches, giving you the choice of 2-by-6 joists that can span 9 feet, 5 inches; 2-by-8 joists that can span 12 feet, 5 inches; etc. In addition, you can increase the length of joists that you use by cantilevering them up to one third of their total permissible span.

MAXIMUM JOIST SPAN

Joist Size	Joist Spacing		
	12"	16"	24"
2 x 6	10'4"	9'5"	7'10"
2 x 8	13'8"	12'5"	10'2"
2 x 10	17'5"	15'5"	12'7"
2 x 12	20'0"	17'10"	14'7"

MAXIMUM BEAM SPAN

Beam Size	Joist Span/Beam Spacing									
	4'	5'	6'	7'	8'	9'	10'	12'	14'	16'
2 x 6s (2)	7'	6'	—	—	—	—	—	—	—	—
2 x 8s (2)	9'	8'	7'	7'	6'	6'	—	—	—	—
2 x 10s (2)	11'	10'	9'	8'	8'	7'	7'	6'	6'	—
2 x 12s (2)	13'	12'	10'	10'	9'	8'	8'	7'	6'	6'

Selecting beam size and spans.

Once the joist spans/beam spacing are determined, use the chart above to figure the sizes and spans of the beams, and thus the post spacing. The figures given are for beams constructed of two pieces of 2-by lumber fastened together, but you can substitute 4-by lumber of the same width. Round up the figure for the joist span/beam spacing to the next interval: For instance, if the joist span is 9 feet, 5 inches, follow the column for a 10-foot joist span; if two 2-by-10s are to be used, the beam span would be 7 feet. Increasing the size of the beams will allow you to increase the beam span, and thus reduce the number of posts needed. Like joists, beams can be cantilevered up to one third of their span.

MAXIMUM POST HEIGHTS

Post Size	Load Area in Square Feet					
	36'	48'	60'	72'	84'	96'
4 x 4	10'	10'	10'	9'	9'	8'
6 x 6	17'	17'	17'	17'	17'	17'

Determining post size and height.

To calculate the load area that each post will have to support, first multiply the joist span by the beam span. Using the chart at left, you can then determine the size of posts required and the maximum height they can extend. For instance, on a deck with a joist span of 9 feet, 5 inches, and a beam span of 7 feet, the load area would be almost 66 square feet. Round this figure up to the next increment, 72 feet. For this load area, you can use 4-by-4 posts for a deck up to 9 feet high. For a higher deck, you must use larger posts or space them closer together. Choose 6-by-6 posts only when 4-by-4s are inadequate.

The stability of a deck depends much on the strength of its foundation, which is built in the first stage of construction. Before you begin, make sure the lot is properly graded to prevent water from pooling around the posts.

Layout: An attached deck *(page 20)* is laid out with one or more string lines parallel to the house that represent the rows of posts *(below)*. A freestanding deck *(page 21)* also employs string lines, with the first one taking the place of the house. For a deck that is not rectangular, a special layout of post locations may be needed *(pages 42-57)*.

Ledgers: On flat siding such as wood panels or brick veneer, a ledger is secured by bolts through the siding and into the house framing *(pages 24-25)*. With overlapping siding such as vinyl or clapboard, a section must be removed so the ledger can lie flat against the sheathing *(page 26)*. For a wall of solid brick, concrete, or concrete block, use masonry anchors to fasten the ledger in place.

Foundations: Decks in a freezing climate must be supported on concrete footings that extend 8 inches below the frost line. Posts can generally be sunk directly into the footings *(page 27)*, but some codes require

that they be set in metal bases cast into the footings *(pages 28-29)*. Post bases are also needed for a low-level deck where beams rest directly on the footings. In a frost-free climate, posts can be supported by precast concrete pier blocks *(page 29)*.

When a deck plan includes continuous posts for an overhead or railing *(page 35)*, use post lumber that is long enough to extend the height of the railing or overhead.

CAUTION *Before digging footing holes, establish the location of underground utilities such as electric, water, and sewer lines.*

 TOOLS

Mason's line	Hammer
Maul	Socket wrench
Chalk line	Wood chisel
Plumb bob	Tin snips
Powdered chalk	Caulking gun
Carpenter's level (4')	Post-hole digger
Circular saw	Shovel
Electric drill	Concrete tools
	Utility knife

 MATERIALS

1 x 2s, 1 x 4, 2 x 2s, 2 x 4	Post bases
Pressure-treated lumber for ledgers and posts	Framing-anchor nails
Exterior plywood ($\frac{1}{2}$")	Galvanized nails ($3\frac{1}{2}$")
Wood preservative	Galvanized lag screws ($\frac{3}{8}$" x $3\frac{1}{2}$") and washers
Roofing felt	Metal flashing
	Silicone sealant
	Concrete mix
	Fiber form tubes

SAFETY TIPS

Wear goggles when using power tools or hammering. Add gloves to work with concrete or metal flashing. Put on a dust mask when cutting pressure-treated wood; wash your hands thoroughly after handling the wood.

DEFINING THE LAYOUT

1. Starting the layout.

◆ Make a mark on the wall representing one end of the deck—in this example, an attached deck with cantilevered joists that ends at the corner of the house.
◆ From the mark, measure along the wall the amount of the planned beam overhang to position the outside of the corner post and tap a nail partway into the wall at this point.
◆ Measure an additional 6 feet along the wall and tap in a second nail.

◆ Tie a length of mason's line longer than the deck's planned width to the first nail and the other end to a 2-by-2 stake. Mark this cord 8 feet from the wall.
◆ Tie a length of mason's line to the second nail and mark it at 10 feet.
◆ Working with a helper, pull the lines taut and maneuver them until the marked points meet *(right)*, then drive the stake into the ground with a maul.
◆ Repeat the process at the other end of the deck.

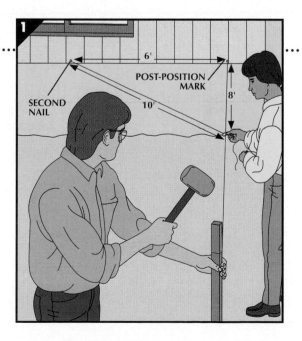

2. Locating the posts.

◆ For every planned row of posts, mark both string lines with masking tape where the outside faces of the posts will lie.

◆ Put up another string line—with a stake at each end—parallel to the house and crossing the first two lines at the marked points. Add string lines in the same way for any additional rows of posts that will be located underneath the deck.

◆ With a plumb bob, transfer the points where the string lines cross to the ground and mark each point with powdered chalk.

◆ Measure along the string lines to place any additional posts and mark these points on the ground *(right)*.

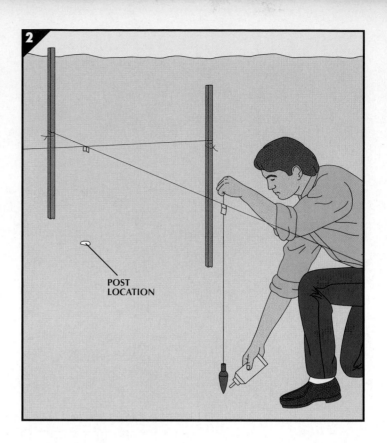

POST
LOCATION

ATTACHING A LEDGER TO FLAT SIDING

1. Locating the ledger.

◆ Make a mark for the top of the ledger 3 inches below the door threshold—or, if you are planning to add a platform to the deck *(pages 52-53)*, lower the ledger accordingly.

◆ Cut a straight 2-by-6 to the length of the deck, minus 3 inches to allow for the joists that will cover the ends of the ledger.

◆ With a helper, hold the ledger against the house with the top edge in line with the mark you just made. Place a 4-foot carpenter's level on top of the board and level it.

◆ Make a mark along the top of the ledger near each end *(left)*, then remove the ledger and snap a chalk line between the marks.

For a very large deck requiring more than one ledger board, instead of holding up the boards, establish the ledger height with a water level.

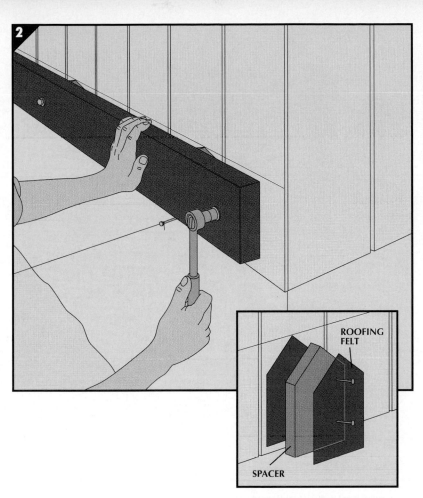

ROOFING FELT

SPACER

2. Installing the board.

◆ From $\frac{1}{2}$-inch exterior plywood, cut pointed spacers 3 inches wide and the height of the ledger board; soak them in wood preservative overnight. For each spacer, cut two pieces of roofing felt of the same shape and sandwich the spacer between the two layers of felt.

◆ Position a spacer 2 inches in from the mark indicating the edge of the deck, with its tip just below the ledger-location line; tack the spacer to the wall with two $3\frac{1}{2}$-inch galvanized common or spiral-shank nails *(inset)*. Fasten additional spacers every 2 feet along the chalk line.

◆ With a helper, lift the ledger into place, aligning it with the chalk line and centering it between the marks indicating the edge of the deck. Tack the ledger to the spacers.

◆ At each spacer location, drill a $\frac{3}{8}$-inch clearance hole through the ledger, then drive a $\frac{3}{8}$- by $3\frac{1}{2}$-inch lag screw fitted with a flat washer through each hole *(left)* and into the framing of the house *(box, below)*.

◆ Cover the lag-screw heads with silicone sealant.

FASTENING TO VARIOUS KINDS OF FRAMING

For a ledger to provide solid support to a deck, it must be attached securely to the house framing. If the deck falls above floor height, simply locate wall studs and fasten the ledger to them with lag screws. In most cases where the deck is the same height as the floor, the ledger can be fastened with lag screws to the solid wood of the floor joist at the side of the house *(near right)*. Some houses, however, are built with I-beams or trusses, which must be reinforced before a ledger can be attached. To do so, you must first expose the inner sides of the I-beam or truss where the ledger will sit. Cut away the ceiling in the room below, making an opening about 2 feet wide along the proposed location of the ledger.

For an I-beam, reinforce the beam inside and outside with boards the full length of the ledger *(center, right)*: Measure the distance between the flanges of the I-beam and select 2-inch boards to fit. Working through holes in the ceiling, tack them to the plywood web. Outside, cut away the sheathing to expose the web, then secure the boards to it with carriage bolts and nail the strip of sheathing back in place. Attach the ledger to the assembly with lag screws.

For a truss, strengthen a section at least as long as the ledger with boards that match the height of the truss *(far right)*: Attach the boards to the truss with 3-inch nails and fasten the ledger to these boards with carriage bolts.

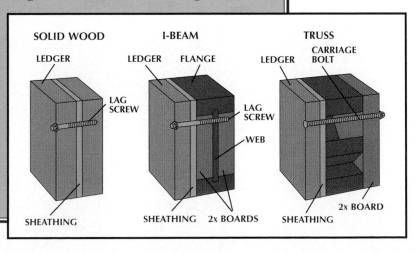

SOLID WOOD

LEDGER

LAG SCREW

SHEATHING

I-BEAM

LEDGER   FLANGE

LAG SCREW

WEB

SHEATHING   2x BOARDS

TRUSS

CARRIAGE BOLT

LEDGER

2x BOARD

SHEATHING

FASTENING TO OVERLAPPING SIDING

EDGE OF DECK

1. Cutting away the siding.

◆ Mark the top of the ledger board as on page 24, Step 1, allowing an extra 3 inches for the joists that will cover its ends. Also snap a chalk line for the bottom of the ledger, plus 3 inches.

◆ With a carpenter's level, extend the marks indicating the edges of the deck so that they cross both horizontal lines.

◆ Set the blade of a circular saw to the siding depth (for aluminum siding, equip the saw with a metal-cutting blade) and cut along the top and bottom lines *(left)*.

◆ Tack a 1-by-4 along a vertical end mark to create a flat surface for the saw to ride on. Adjust the saw-blade depth and make the vertical cut, letting the saw's base plate ride on top of the 1-by-4; then repeat the cut at the other end of the outline.

◆ Complete the corners with a wood chisel—or tin snips for aluminum.

◆ Work the section of siding away from the wall, using a pry bar with a wood block under it for leverage, if necessary.

2. Installing flashing.

◆ With tin snips, cut enough strips of 7-inch-wide metal flashing to span the opening in the siding, then bend each one lengthwise 4 inches from an edge.

◆ Push the 4-inch leg of one piece of flashing under the siding, cutting slots for any siding nails.

◆ Continue to install strips of flashing to fill the opening, overlapping the strips by about 2 inches *(right)*.

◆ Fasten the ledger as on page 25—but without spacers.

◆ Bend the flashing down over the face of the ledger with a hammer and a block of wood.

◆ With silicone sealant, caulk the screw holes, the joints between pieces of flashing, the joint between the flashing and siding, and the joint between the bottom of the ledger and the siding.

FLASHING

SETTING POSTS IN CONCRETE

1. Making the footings.
◆ Remove the string lines.
◆ With a post-hole digger, dig a hole at each chalked post location *(right)*, making the holes 10 inches across at the top, widening to 16 inches at the bottom; and 24 inches deep or 8 inches below the frost line, whichever is deeper. Since footings must rest on undisturbed soil, do not backfill the holes with loose earth.
◆ Mix concrete *(page 17)* and pour 8 inches of it into each hole.

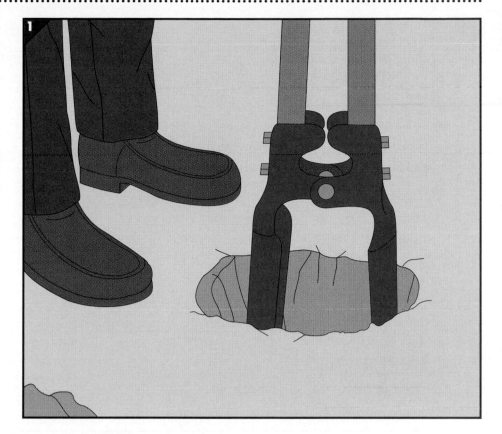

BRACE

POST

2. Setting the posts.
◆ Retie the string lines.
◆ Cut a post long enough to extend above the ground by a few inches more than its final height. If the deck plan includes continuous posts for a railing or overhead *(page 35)*, use uncut posts at least as long as the required height.
◆ Set the post in the hole with its uncut end down, and position it at the inter-section of the strings. Fasten a 1-by-2 brace to one side of the post with a single nail, then drive a stake into the ground within reach of the brace.
◆ Have a helper plumb the post with a carpenter's level, then nail the brace to the stake, backing up the stake with a maul *(left)*. Plumb and brace an adja-cent side of the post, then set and plumb the remaining posts in the same way.
◆ Fill the holes with concrete to within a few inches of the lip.
◆ After the concrete has set for at least 24 hours, remove the braces and pack the hollows with earth, sloping the surface away from the posts.

USING METAL POST BASES

FIBER FORM
TUBE

1. Inserting fiber tubes.

◆ Dig a hole and pour a footing for each post (page 27, Step 1).

◆ With a handsaw, cut an 8-inch-diameter fiber form tube long enough to reach the bottom of the hole and extend 2 inches above the ground. Insert the tube in the hole (above) and center it. Fill in around the outside of the tube with about a foot of earth to stabilize it.

◆ Cut and insert the remaining tubes.

◆ If you will be setting beams directly on the piers, put two to three shovelfuls of concrete into each tube, then level the tubes (Step 2). Otherwise, fill all the tubes with concrete and smooth the top of each one with a scrap piece of 2-by-4, then proceed immediately to Step 3.

2. Leveling the tubes.

◆ Set a straight board across an adjacent pair of tubes and place a 4-foot carpenter's level on top of the board. Note which tube is higher. Continue checking adjacent tubes in the same way until you locate the highest one.

◆ Placing the board and level on the highest tube and an adjacent one, pull up on the lower tube until the board is level (above). Continue to adjust the tubes so that each is level with one you have previously leveled.

◆ Add concrete to fill all the tubes, then smooth the top of each by pulling a scrap piece of 2-by-4 across the top of the tube.

TRICKS OF THE TRADE

Pier and Footings in One

Instead of shoveling concrete for the wide footing into each hole, then inserting and filling the tubes to form the piers, you can cast the footings and piers in one shot. Cut a tube to run from 8 inches above the bottom of the hole to 2 inches above the surface. Nail opposite sides of the tube to two 2-by-4s. Set the tube in the hole suspended from the 2-by-4s and center it. With the 2-by-4s held in place with small stakes, the concrete can be poured.

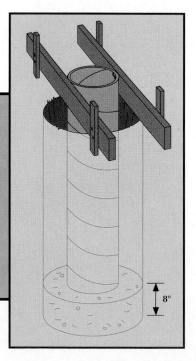

8"

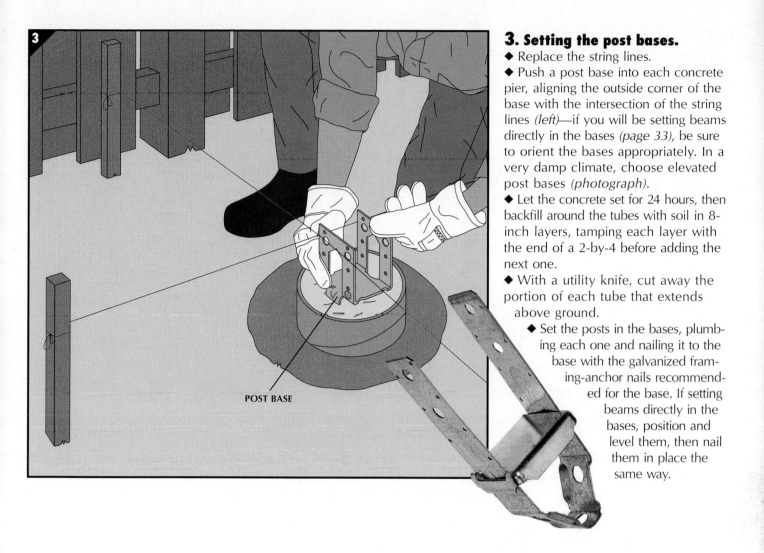

POST BASE

3. Setting the post bases.

◆ Replace the string lines.

◆ Push a post base into each concrete pier, aligning the outside corner of the base with the intersection of the string lines *(left)*—if you will be setting beams directly in the bases *(page 33)*, be sure to orient the bases appropriately. In a very damp climate, choose elevated post bases *(photograph)*.

◆ Let the concrete set for 24 hours, then backfill around the tubes with soil in 8-inch layers, tamping each layer with the end of a 2-by-4 before adding the next one.

◆ With a utility knife, cut away the portion of each tube that extends above ground.

◆ Set the posts in the bases, plumbing each one and nailing it to the base with the galvanized framing-anchor nails recommended for the base. If setting beams directly in the bases, position and level them, then nail them in place the same way.

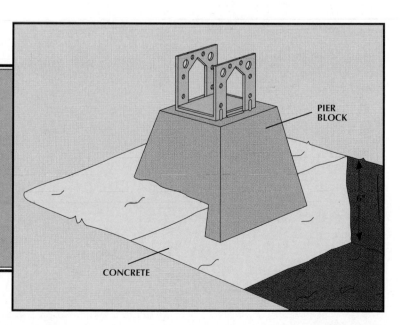

PIER BLOCK

CONCRETE

PIER BLOCKS FOR A WARM CLIMATE
....

In a climate that does not experience frost, deck posts can be supported with precast concrete pier blocks that contain post bases. To set each block, pour a 6-inch-thick concrete pad on undisturbed soil a few inches larger all around than the block, then simply press the block 2 inches down into the wet concrete.

Once the foundation is in place, the beams can be installed. On an attached deck *(page 20)* they run parallel to the house, while on a freestanding deck *(page 21)* you can set them in either direction.

Lumber: Beams can be cut from 4-by lumber. This size gives a solid look to the deck, and allows the beam to sit squarely on top of the posts. If pressure-treated lumber this thickness is not available in your area, you can make a built-up beam by fastening together a pair of 2-by boards.

Attaching Beams: The standard method for attaching a beam to posts is with metal connectors *(opposite, Step 1)*. For a built-up beam, however, you will need to use adjustable post caps since the combined thickness of the boards is $\frac{1}{2}$ inch less than a 4-by-4 post. On a ground-level deck, beams can be set directly in post bases cast into piers *(page 33)*. For

posts cut from 6-by-6s, notch them to receive the beam *(page 34)*. An alternative method is to sandwich two beams around a post *(page 34)*. Though slightly weaker than beams seated on the posts, this design permits you to extend posts upward to support railings or overheads *(page 35)*. It also simplifies the job of cutting the posts to height.

Before fastening the beams to the posts, make sure that the ends of the assembly are aligned *(page 32, Step 2)*.

Bracing Posts: Cross braces between the posts and beams add rigidity to the deck *(page 35)*. Bracing requirements vary depending on local building codes, but in general it is a good idea to use bracing on a freestanding deck more than about 3 feet high, an attached deck higher than about 4 feet, or any deck that projects a long distance from the house.

 TOOLS

Carpenter's level	Circular saw
Chalk line	Handsaw
Combination square	Reciprocating saw
Carpenter's square	Electric drill
	Hammer
	Wrenches

 **MATERIALS**

Pressure-treated lumber for beams and braces
Cedar shims
Post caps
Framing-anchor nails
Common nails ($3\frac{1}{2}$")

Galvanized spiral-shank nails (3", $3\frac{1}{2}$")
Galvanized carriage bolts ($\frac{1}{2}$" x 6", 7") and washers
Galvanized lag screws ($\frac{3}{8}$" x 4") and washers

 SAFETY TIPS

Put on goggles when hammering or using power tools. Wear a dust mask when cutting pressure-treated wood; wash your hands thoroughly after handling the wood.

PREPARING THE POSTS

1. Marking the end posts.

For a deck with a ledger, have a helper set one end of a straight piece of lumber on top of the ledger. Rest the other end against an end post, then level the board and mark the post along its bottom edge *(right)*.
◆ Measure down the post the height of a joist and the height of a beam, then make a mark at this point to indicate the top of the post *(inset)*. For a 6-by-6 post or a split beam *(page 34)*, measure down only the height of a joist.
◆ Mark the other end post in the same way.

For a freestanding deck, measure up from the ground to mark one post, then transfer the measurements to the other posts with a water level.

TOP OF JOIST
TOP OF BEAM
TOP OF POST

2. Marking intermediate posts.

◆ Tap a nail into the face of one end post, level with the post-height mark, and hook the end of a chalk line over the nail. Unwind the chalk line and hold it level with the post-height mark on the other end post. Snap the line to mark the intermediary posts *(right)*.
◆ With a combination square, draw a line around all the faces of each post level with the post-height mark.
◆ Unless you will be installing a split beam *(page 34)*, cut off the top of the posts along the marked lines with a circular saw.

THE STANDARD METHOD OF PLACING BEAMS

CUT-OFF CORNER

ADJUSTABLE POST CAP

1. Seating the beams.

◆ With galvanized framing-anchor nails, fasten a post cap to the top of each post. Use standard caps for a solid 4-by beam, adjustable caps set 3 inches apart for a built-up beam of 2-bys.
◆ Cut a 4-by beam to the desired length; or, make a built-up beam: Fasten together two pieces of 2-by lumber the length of the deck, driving 3-inch galvanized spiral-shank nails in rows of three at 16-inch intervals. Turn over the assembly and nail in the same pattern, positioning rows to fall midway between those on the opposite side.
◆ On each end of the beam, make marks 2 inches from a corner on the end and the bottom, then draw a diagonal line joining them. Cut along the line with a circular saw.
◆ Working with a helper, sit the beam in the post caps with the cut-off corners at the ends facing down *(left)*.

2. Nailing the beam.

◆ Adjust the position of the beam to allow for the correct amount of overhang at each end.

◆ To check that the ends of the beam line up with the ends of the ledger, tack a long straight board to the ledger and set it on the beam. Square the board to the ledger with a carpenter's square and adjust the beam until the end of it is flush with the outside face of the squared board.

◆ Fasten the post caps to the beam with framing-anchor nails *(right)*.

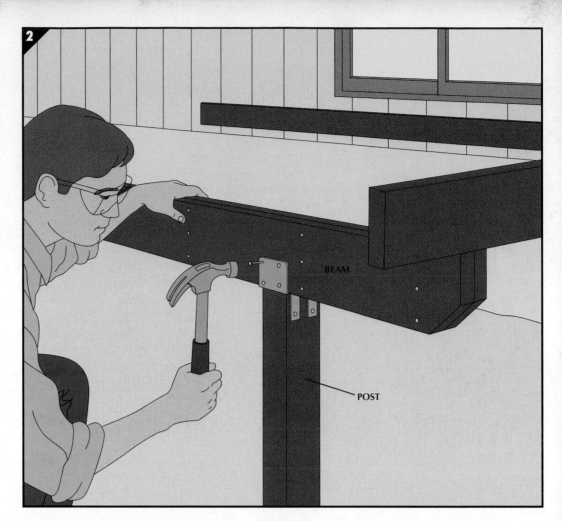

BEAM

POST

SPLICING BEAMS

For a large deck, you may have to splice lumber to make a long-enough beam. For a beam built of two 2-bys, simply stagger the joints between the two faces when joining the pieces, being sure that joints fall over a post *(right)*. For a solid 4-by beam, locate the joint over a post and tie the pieces together with a length of metal strapping nailed across the joint on each side of the beam near the top.

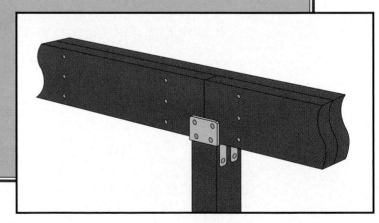

Beams for a low deck.

◆ Working with a helper, set the beam directly into the post bases. If you are using a built-up beam *(page 31, Step 1)*, trim a pair of cedar shims to the height of the beam and insert them on the inner side of the beam between it and the post bases.

◆ Measure the beam to ensure that it overhangs each end pier by the same amount. As described opposite, Step 2, use a long straight board and a carpenter's square to align the ends of the beam and a ledger or of two beams.

◆ Fasten the beams to the bases with galvanized framing-anchor nails *(left)*.

CEDAR SHIMS

DECKING OVER A PATIO

If you want to convert a patio to a deck, you can do it by placing pressure-treated sleepers across the patio, spaced the same distance apart as joists, and laying decking on the sleepers. If the patio is sloped to shed rainwater and the surface is even and in good condition, simply fasten the sleepers to it with glue made for attaching wood to concrete outdoors, then lay the decking in the same way as you would on joists *(pages 62-70)*. For an uneven surface, shim the sleepers with cedar shingles at the low spots, then fasten the sleepers and shims to the patio with glue and masonry anchors.

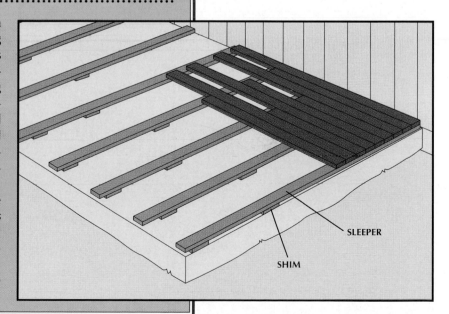

SLEEPER

SHIM

Attaching to 6-by-6 posts.

◆ With a combination square, mark the top of each post for a notch 3 inches deep and as high as the width of the beam lumber you are using—locate the notch on the side of the post facing away from the house.

◆ Set the blade of a circular saw to the maximum cutting depth and cut along the lines, then finish the cuts with a handsaw.

◆ Measure the beam to ensure that it overhangs each end post by the same amount. As described on page 32, Step 2, use a long straight board and a carpenter's square to align the ends of the beam and the ledger or the ends of two beams.

◆ Toenail the beam to each post with $3\frac{1}{2}$-inch galvanized spiral-shank nails.

◆ Drill two $\frac{1}{2}$-inch offset holes through the beam and each post, then install $\frac{1}{2}$- by 6-inch carriage bolts in the holes *(right)*.

POST-HEIGHT MARK

A split beam.

◆ Cut two 2-bys to length to form the beam. Working with a helper, lift one piece into place against the posts with its top edge aligned with the marked lines, checking that the appropriate amount extends past each end post.

◆ Tack each end of the beam to the post with a partially-driven $3\frac{1}{2}$-inch common nail. Fasten the second board to the opposite face of the posts in the same way *(left)*.

◆ As described on page 32, Step 2, use a long straight board and a carpenter's square to check that the ends of the beam line up with the ends of the ledger or other beam.

◆ Drill two $\frac{1}{2}$-inch holes through the beam and each post, then install $\frac{1}{2}$- by 7-inch carriage bolts in the holes and pull out the nails.

◆ Unless the posts will support a railing or overhead *(opposite)*, cut them off flush with the top of the beam using a reciprocating saw—the joists will hide the rough ends.

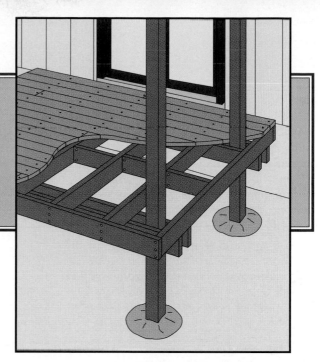

CONTINUOUS POSTS FOR AN OVERHEAD

One advantage of attaching split beams to posts *(opposite)* is that the posts can extend upward to provide solid support for a railing or an overhead. If you design your deck in this manner, you may want to adjust the amount that the beams and joists are cantilevered so that the posts will fall close to the outside edges of the deck.

BRACING POSTS

Attaching the braces.

◆ For posts between 3 and 8 feet tall, cut 2-by-4 braces 3 feet long, making parallel miter cuts at the ends. For taller posts, cut braces from 2-by-6 stock.
◆ Set one end of the brace against the beam and center the lower end on the post. Tack each end in place with a partially-driven $3\frac{1}{2}$-inch nail.
◆ For all but the end posts, attach a second brace, leaving a $\frac{1}{8}$-inch gap between it and the first brace *(left)*.
◆ Add braces to the opposite side of the posts and beams in the same way.
◆ Drill $\frac{1}{2}$-inch clearance holes through the ends of the braces and install $\frac{1}{2}$- by 7-inch carriage bolts, then pull out the nails.

For split beams, 2-by-4 braces fit between the boards making up the beam: Bevel both ends of each brace, tack the brace in place, then fasten it to the beam with a $\frac{1}{2}$- by 7-inch carriage bolt and to the post with a $\frac{3}{8}$- by 4-inch lag screw *(inset)*.

The next phase of the building process is to install joists, which form the framework on which the decking is laid. For an attached deck *(below)*, joists are fastened to the ledger with joist hangers; their other ends rest on the beam and are joined by a rim joist. On a freestanding deck, whose joists are supported by beams at both ends, the end and rim joists are installed first, then the intermediate joists are laid *(page 40)*.

Special Techniques: Most lumber used for deck framing has a slight curve or "crown." Before you install the joists, sight down their edges to detect the curve and lay them crown-up. On a well-crafted deck, the end grain of the framing members is concealed as much as possible. In the design on these pages, the end joists hide the ends of the ledger. If railing posts will cover the joints between the rim and end joists, you can butt the members together, leaving the end grain exposed. Otherwise, bevel the joints *(page 40)* or hide them with a beveled fascia that matches the decking *(page 64)*.

Blocking: Some local codes require blocking *(page 41)* to keep joists from twisting; it is generally placed directly over an inner beam and at the midpoint of joists spanning more than 8 feet. It is also wise to place blocking behind the end joists wherever a railing post will be added.

 TOOLS

Tape measure
Combination
  square
Chalk line

Hammer
Circular saw
Hand plane
Caulking gun

 **MATERIALS**

Pressure-treated lumber for
  joists and blocking
Joist hangers
Multipurpose framing
  anchors

Rafter ties
Framing-anchor nails
Galvanized spiral-shank
  nails ($3\frac{1}{2}$")
Silicone sealant

 SAFETY TIPS

Protect your eyes with goggles when hammering or sawing. Add a dust mask when cutting pressure-treated wood and wash your hands thoroughly after handling the wood.

AN ATTACHED DECK

1. Installing the end joists.
◆ Cut an end joist a few inches longer than the planned width of the deck.
◆ Set the joist in place with one end resting on the outer beam and the other against the end of the ledger.
◆ With $3\frac{1}{2}$-inch galvanized spiral-shank nails, fasten the end joist to the ledger so the upper edges are flush *(right)*.
◆ Where you have cut away siding, seal the joint between the end joist and the siding with silicone sealant.

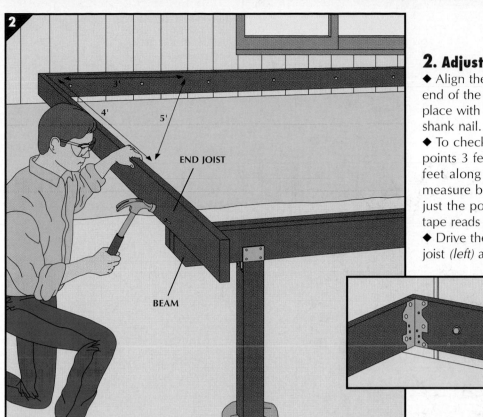

2. Adjusting for square.

◆ Align the joist's outer face with the end of the beam and tack the joist in place with a 3½-inch galvanized spiral-shank nail.

◆ To check the joist for square, mark points 3 feet along the ledger and 4 feet along the joist. Stretch a tape measure between the marks and adjust the position of the joist until the tape reads 5 feet.

◆ Drive the nail all the way into the joist *(left)* and reinforce the inside corner at the ledger with a galvanized multipurpose framing anchor *(inset)*.

◆ Install the end joist on the opposite side in the same manner.

3. Marking the joist locations.

◆ Starting from one end joist, measure along the ledger and mark joist locations at the appropriate spacing *(chart, page 22)*. The last joist location may fall closer to the end of the ledger than the standard distance.

◆ With a combination square, draw a vertical line on the face of the ledger in line with a mark *(right)*, then draw an X on the side of the line where the joist will be attached.

◆ Outline the remaining joist locations, then mark the top face of the outermost beam in the same way, beginning the layout at the same end that you did for the ledger.

4. Installing joist hangers.

◆ Position a joist hanger on the ledger at the first location line so the opening falls over the X.

◆ Set a scrap piece of joist lumber in the hanger and adjust the height of the hanger so the block is flush with the top of the ledger.

◆ With galvanized framing-anchor nails, fasten the joist hanger on the side next to the line. Squeeze the hanger snug around the block of wood and nail the opposite side. Install joist hangers at the remaining location lines in the same way *(right)*.

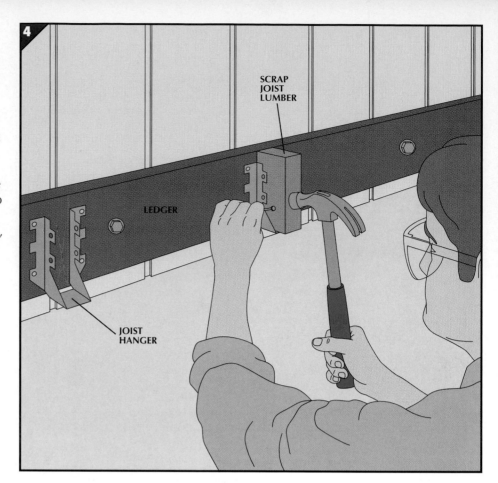

SPLICING JOISTS

If you are building a large deck, you may not be able to purchase joist stock long enough to span the distance from the ledger to the outermost beam. In this case, splice joists together over a central beam by overlapping them 12 inches and nailing them together with 3-inch galvanized spiral-shank nails. Be sure to take into account the staggered layout when marking the joist locations on the ledger and beams. Whenever possible, avoid placing all the splices over the same beam.

Since an overlapping splice on an end joist would be visible, butt the joist sections end-to-end instead and reinforce the splice with a 1-foot length of joist lumber nailed across the inner side of the joint.

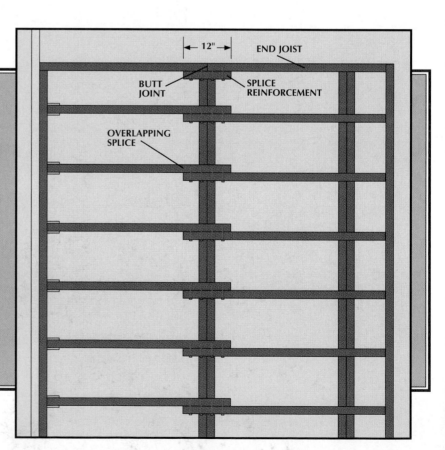

5. Trimming the joists.

◆ Set a joist a few inches longer than the planned width of the deck into the joist hanger next to the end joist and fasten it in place with galvanized framing-anchor nails.

◆ Install the remaining joists in the same way.

◆ Align a joist with its mark on the beam and toenail it in place, or attach it with a rafter tie *(photograph)* where required by code.

◆ Fasten the remaining joists to the beam in the same way.

◆ Along each end joist, measure from the house the planned width of the deck less $1\frac{1}{2}$ inches and make a mark.

◆ Tap in a nail at one of the marks and slip the end of a chalk line over the nail. Stretch the line to the mark on the other end joist and snap the line *(left)*.

◆ With a combination square, transfer the mark on each joist to the face of the joist, then trim the joists along the lines with a circular saw.

6. Adding the rim joist.

◆ Cut a rim joist to the length of the deck, or splice one to fit *(page 40, box)*. Working with a helper, hold it in place against the ends of the joists flush with the outer sides of the end joists and fasten it to one of the end joists with three galvanized $3\frac{1}{2}$-inch spiral-shank nails.

◆ Have your helper raise or lower the rim joist so it is flush with the next joist, then nail it in place. Continue fastening the rim joist to the end of each joist, raising and lowering it as needed *(right)*.

RIM JOIST

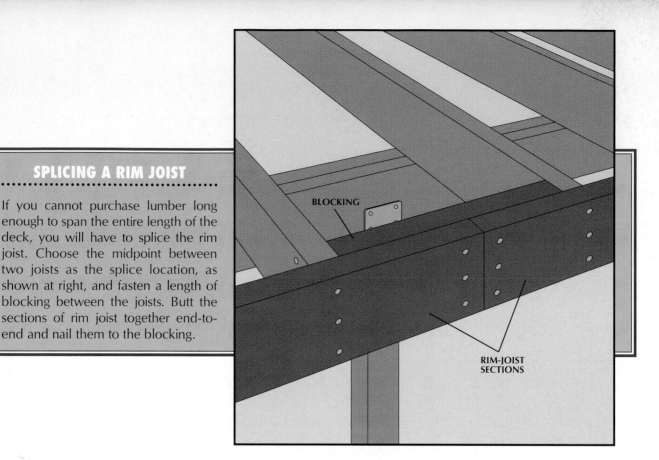

SPLICING A RIM JOIST

If you cannot purchase lumber long enough to span the entire length of the deck, you will have to splice the rim joist. Choose the midpoint between two joists as the splice location, as shown at right, and fasten a length of blocking between the joists. Butt the sections of rim joist together end-to-end and nail them to the blocking.

BLOCKING

RIM-JOIST SECTIONS

A FREESTANDING DECK

Installing the framing.

◆ Cut two end joists to length, beveling the ends.

◆ Position one piece across the beams so it over-hangs them by the same amount at both ends.

◆ Cut two rim joists, beveling the ends to fit the end joists. Working with a helper, lift the rim joist into place and fasten each beveled corner with three nails. Install the second rim joist in the same way.

◆ Measure the deck diagonally from corner to corner; if the diagonals are not equal, tap the frame with a hammer to square it.

◆ Toenail the end joists to the beams with $3\frac{1}{2}$-inch galvanized spiral-shank nails.

◆ Round the frame's beveled corners slightly with a hand plane.

◆ Mark the joist locations on the rim joists as you would on a ledger *(page 37, Step 2)*.

◆ Cut the intermediate joists and lift each one into place, align it with the marks, and fasten it to the rim joists with three nails *(right)*. Toenail the joists to the beam or install rafter ties if required by code *(page 39, Step 5)*.

END JOIST

RIM JOIST

BEAM

ADDING BLOCKING

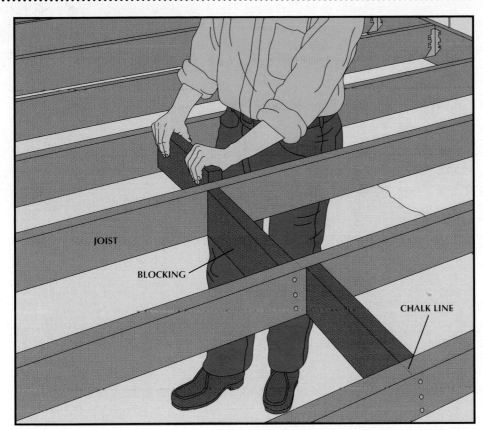

Fitting in blocking.
◆ If codes require blocking *(page 36)*, cut a piece to fit between each pair of joists from lumber of the same size.
◆ Snap a chalk line across the joists in the middle of the deck or over a beam, as the code indicates.
◆ Fit the blocking between the joists, placing consecutive pieces on opposite sides of the chalk line *(left)*, and fasten it to the joists with three $3\frac{1}{2}$-inch galvanized spiral-shank nails at each end.

(page 36)

BLOCKING FOR RAILINGS

Where an intermediate railing post *(dashed lines)* will be attached to an end joist *(page 83)*, it is a good idea to reinforce the joist with blocking. Cut a length of blocking and fasten it between the joists as described above, placing it about 4 inches from the planned railing-post location.

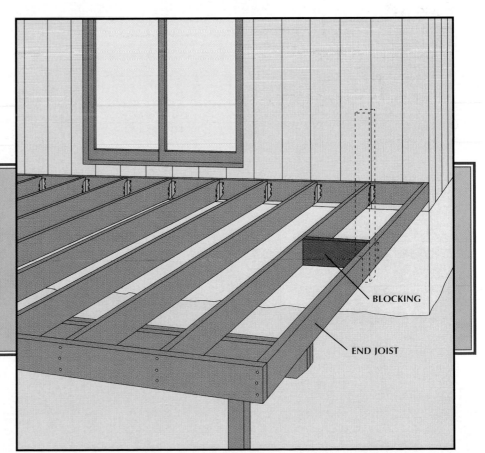

Although a rectangular deck is the easiest type to build, altering this shape can add visual interest. Variations include cutting the corners at an angle or wrapping the deck around two sides of the house. You can also incorporate a natural element of the landscape such as a tree or rock, or add a curve at the corners *(pages 69-71)*.

A Cut-Off Corner: You can create a small angled corner by cutting the end and rim joists short and linking the two sides with a board. For a large angle, you'll need to cut one or more of the intermediate joists and add a short beam to support them *(below)*.

A Wraparound Deck: The framing design for a wraparound deck is dependent on the type of decking you plan to install. One of the most common arrangements is to extend a double joist straight out from the corner of the house *(pages 45-48)* and miter the decking where it meets at the joist *(page 66)*, but you can also plan the framing to support parallel decking *(page 48, box)*.

Natural Features: Rather than removing trees or rocks that lie within the perimeter of the deck, you can leave them in place to integrate the deck with its surroundings and enhance its natural charm. To do so, you must first frame an opening in the substructure *(pages 49-51)*; the decking can then be cut to follow the shape of the object *(page 71)*.

 TOOLS

Tape measure
Mason's line
Maul
Chalk line
Combination square
Circular saw
Reciprocating saw
Electric drill
Hammer
Socket wrench
Hand plane
Post-hole digger
Shovel
Concrete tools

 MATERIALS

2 x 2s
Materials for casting footings and setting posts
Pressure-treated lumber for ledgers, posts, beams, joists, and other framing
Post caps
Multipurpose framing anchors
Joist hangers
Framing-anchor nails
Galvanized lag screws ($\frac{3}{8}$" x $3\frac{1}{2}$") and washers
Galvanized spiral-shank nails ($3\frac{1}{2}$")
Galvanized common nails (3")

SAFETY TIPS

Put on goggles when using a power tool or hammering. Wear a dust mask to cut pressure-treated lumber and wash your hands thoroughly after handling the wood.

A CUT-OFF CORNER

Anatomy of an angled corner.
In this design, the rim and end joists, as well as two intermediate joists, are cut at an angle and linked with a short rim joist beveled to fit the angle. The end post of the main beam is set back farther than usual from the edge of the deck and the corner is buttressed by a short extra beam set on two posts.

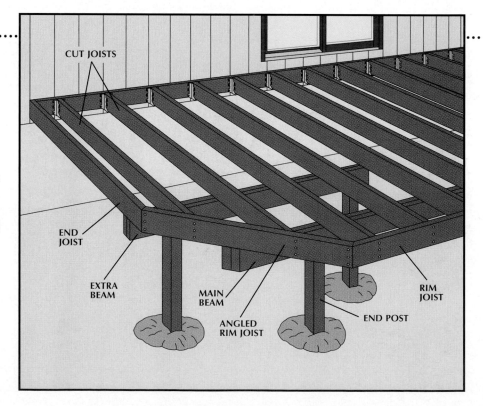

1. Cutting end and rim joists.

◆ Cast footings and set posts and beams *(pages 23-35)*, placing the end post of the main beam far enough from the edge of the deck to accommodate the corner and adding a short beam to support the joists to be cut short.

◆ Install the joists and rim joist *(pages 36-40)*, but omit the intermediate joists that will be shortened.

◆ Mark the end joist at the desired distance from the corner and the rim joist at the same measurement.

◆ Set the blade of a circular saw to $22\frac{1}{2}$ degrees and trim the end joist at the mark *(left)*—angle the cut so the outside face of the joist is longer than the inside one.

◆ Bevel the rim joist in the same way.

2. Trimming the main beam.

◆ Measure the distance between the beveled ends of the rim and end joists and cut a short length of rim joist to fit, angling the ends at $22\frac{1}{2}$ degrees.

◆ Have a helper hold the joist in place, and mark where it crosses the main beam *(right)*. Remove the angled rim joist and, with a combination square, transfer the cutting line to the faces of the beam. With a reciprocating saw, trim the beam along the lines.

◆ Fit the angled joist back in place and nail it to both the end and rim joists with three $3\frac{1}{2}$-inch galvanized spiral-shank nails.

◆ Round the beveled corners slightly with a hand plane.

3. Locating the cut joists.

◆ Hook a tape measure over the last full-length joist, positioning it parallel to the rim joist and across the angled rim joist at a point equal to the joist spacing; mark the angled joist at this location *(left)*.

◆ Record the location of the remaining joists on the angled rim joist in the same way.

◆ Measure the distance between each joist hanger on the ledger to the corresponding mark on the angled rim joist and cut a joist to fit, beveling one end at 45 degrees.

◆ Install the cut joists, fastening them to the joist hangers with galvanized framing-anchor nails and to the angled rim joist with three $3\frac{1}{2}$-inch galvanized spiral-shank nails.

LEDGER

ANGLED RIM JOIST

RIM JOIST

AN OCTAGONAL DECK

By angling all four corners of a square free-standing deck, you can create an octagonal design *(right)*. For the framing, use the methods for building a standard deck, but set additional posts and beams to support the shortened joists at the corners.

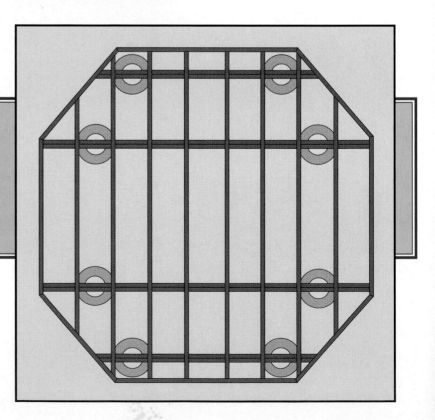

Turning a corner.

In this design, the deck is supported by ledgers fastened to adjoining walls and by beams running parallel to the ledgers. The beams meet at the corner, with their end posts located 18 inches from the corner. A double joist runs from the intersection of the rim joists to the joint between the ledgers, and cripple joists are set between the rim joists and the double joist.

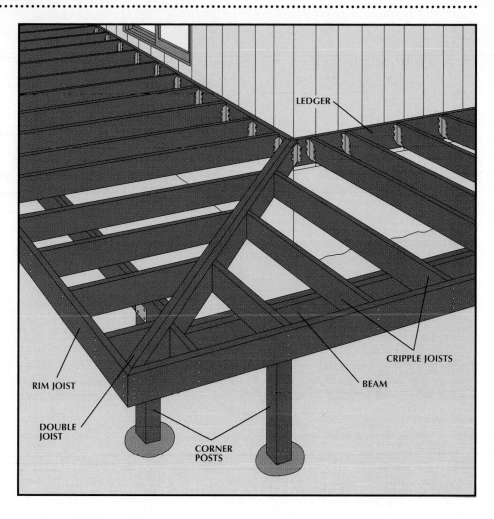

LEDGER

CRIPPLE JOISTS

BEAM

RIM JOIST

DOUBLE JOIST

CORNER POSTS

1. Laying out the deck.

◆ Lay out each section of the deck in the same way as for an ordinary deck *(pages 23-24)*, but when you set up the string lines for the beams at the corner of the deck, extend the lines until they cross *(left)*.
◆ Set posts in the same locations as for an ordinary deck *(page 24)*, but start at the intersection of the corner-beam lines and measure back 18 inches along each line to mark the location of a corner post *(inset)*.

CORNER-BEAM LINES

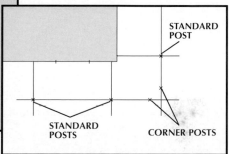

STANDARD POST

STANDARD POSTS

CORNER POSTS

2. Installing the ledgers.

◆ Install a ledger along one wall of the house as for an ordinary deck *(pages 24-26)*, extending it to the corner of the house.

◆ Install a second ledger along the adjoining wall of the house so the end overlaps the first ledger *(right)*.

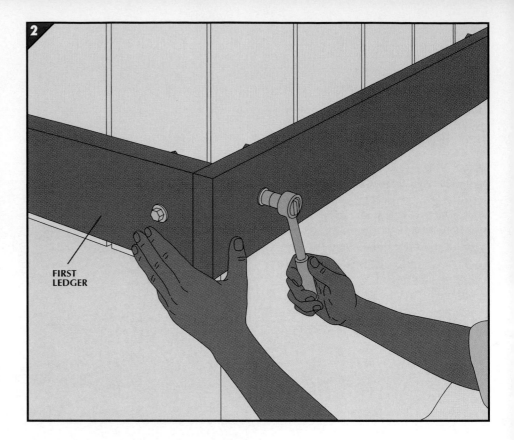

FIRST LEDGER

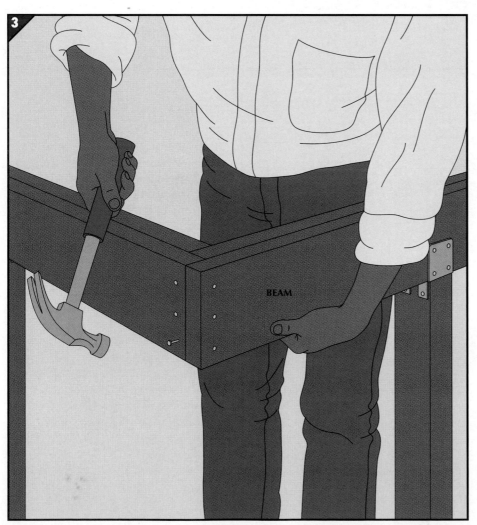

BEAM

3. Setting the beams.

◆ Make two built-up beams as described on page 31, but cut the outer boards $1\frac{1}{2}$ inches longer than the inner boards and fasten them together flush at one end. (If you're working with solid beams, bevel one end of each beam at 45 degrees).

◆ Set the beams in place on the posts so that they interlock at the corner and tie them together with three $3\frac{1}{2}$-inch galvanized spiral-shank nails driven through each side of the joint *(left)*.

◆ Fasten the beams to the post caps with galvanized framing-anchor nails *(page 32)*.

4. Capping the joists.

◆ Install an end joist on each section of the deck *(pages 36-37)*.

◆ Lay out and install the remaining joists *(pages 37-38)*, starting at the house corner and placing the first joist 6 inches from the end of the ledger. Trim the joists on each section of the deck *(page 39)*.

◆ Cut two rim joists long enough to meet at the corner, beveling the ends that will meet. Install the rim joists as described on pages 39-40.

◆ Tie the two rim joists together with three $3\frac{1}{2}$-inch nails driven through each side of the joint *(right)*.

◆ Round the miter joint slightly with a hand plane.

RIM JOIST

5. Fitting in the double joist.

◆ Measure from the corner of the ledger to the inside corner formed by the rim joists. Cut two joists to this length, beveling both ends of each piece at 45 degrees with cuts that are parallel.

◆ With 3-inch galvanized common nails spaced every 16 inches, fasten the two joists together so that the bevels form a V at one end and a point at the other *(inset)*.

◆ Fit the double joist in place between the corner of the house and the rim joists. Fasten it to the ledgers with two multipurpose framing anchors and galvanized framing-anchor nails *(left)*. Fasten it to the rim joists with three $3\frac{1}{2}$-inch galvanized spiral-shank nails driven through each rim joist, then toenail it to the beams.

MULTIPURPOSE
FRAMING
ANCHOR

DOUBLE
JOIST

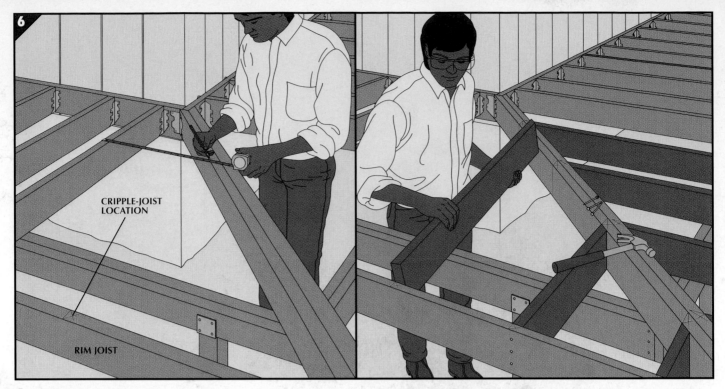

CRIPPLE-JOIST
LOCATION

RIM JOIST

6. Filling in with cripple joists.

◆ Beginning at the joist closest to the corner, lay out locations for the cripple joists along each rim joist, spacing them at the same intervals as the other joists. With a combination square, transfer the marks to the face of the rim joist.

◆ Working near the house wall, hook a measuring tape on the joist closest to the corner so it is parallel to the house and crosses the double joist at a distance from the ledger equal to the joist spacing. Mark the double joist at this point (above, left), then mark the location of the remaining cripple joists on the double joist in the same way.

◆ Transfer the marks to the face of the double joist with a combination square.

◆ Cut cripple joists to fit between the double joist and the rim joist, beveling the ends that will meet the double joist. Set each cripple joist into place (above, right), fastening one end with three $3\frac{1}{2}$-inch galvanized spiral-shank nails driven through the rim joist and toenailing the other end to the double joist with three nails. Finally, toenail the cripple joists to the beams.

A WRAPAROUND DECK WITH PARALLEL DECKING

On a wraparound deck, instead of mitering the decking boards at the corner you can create a seamless look by laying the decking in one direction only. To do so, you must frame the deck in a slightly different manner to support the parallel deck boards. Build one section of the deck in the usual way, with a ledger and beam parallel to the house and joists running perpendicular to it. On the adjacent side of the house, attach a ledger placed one joist-height lower than the first ledger. Hang the beams from this second ledger with double-joist hangers and set the joists on top of the ledger and beams so that they run parallel to the joists on the first section. Overlap the joists as necessary (page 38, box), and splice the rim joists where needed (page 40, box).

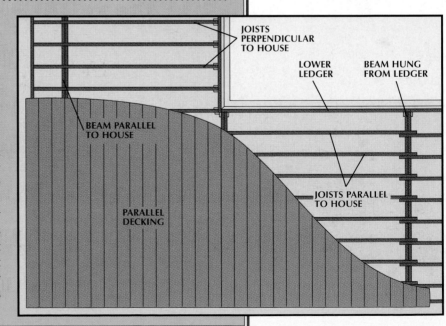

JOISTS PERPENDICULAR TO HOUSE

LOWER LEDGER

BEAM HUNG FROM LEDGER

BEAM PARALLEL TO HOUSE

JOISTS PARALLEL TO HOUSE

PARALLEL DECKING

BUILDING AROUND AN OBSTRUCTION

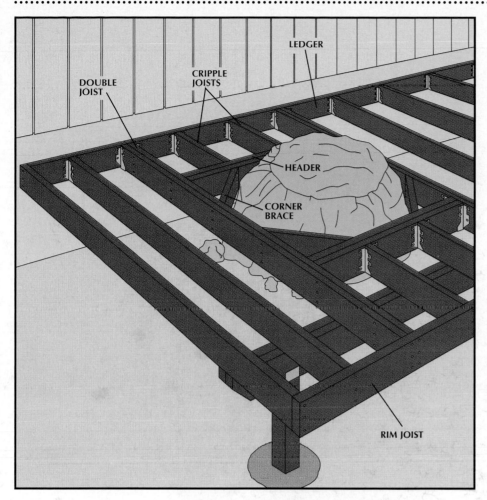

DOUBLE JOIST

CRIPPLE JOISTS

LEDGER

HEADER

CORNER BRACE

RIM JOIST

A reinforced opening.
An opening in a deck that accommodates an obstruction is framed in a specific way to support the joists that must be shortened. First, the joists at each side of the opening are doubled and headers made of doubled joist lumber are fastened to them. Cripple joists are then fastened with joist hangers between the headers and the ledger and rim joist, and the decking is laid over the frame.

Decking can overhang this framing by a maximum of 4 inches. If the opening is large and round—such as for a tree or boulder *(left)*—the deck boards may need to extend by more than 4 inches in some places. In this case, you will need to install corner braces to support the ends of the deck boards. When you frame around a tree, leave a gap of at least 5 inches between the decking and the trunk to give the tree room to grow.

A TREE AS A CENTERPIECE

An enormous oak was growing right in the middle of the planned location of this deck. Instead of cutting down the tree, the owners simply built the deck around it. Plenty of room was left between the deck and the tree to allow for growth, and benches *(pages 100-107)* were added to take advantage of the shade.

1. Hanging double joists.

◆ Install a ledger and set posts and beams as you would for an ordinary deck *(pages 23-35)*.

◆ Lay out joist locations along the ledger and install joist hangers *(pages 36-38)*; use double-joist hangers where the double joists will fall. Transfer the joist locations to the beam.

◆ Install the single joists, omitting those that would cross the obstruction, then add the rim joist.

◆ For each double joist, cut two pieces of joist lumber to length and nail each pair together with rows of three 3-inch galvanized common nails spaced every 16 inches.

◆ Lift the double joist into place and fasten it to the joist hanger with galvanized framing-anchor nails *(right)* and to the rim joist with three $3\frac{1}{2}$-inch galvanized spiral-shank nails. Toenail the double joist to the beam.

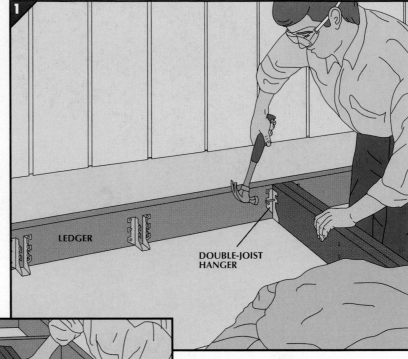

LEDGER

DOUBLE-JOIST HANGER

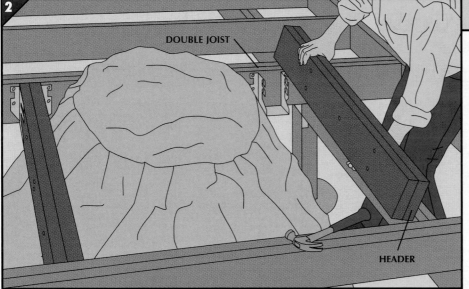

DOUBLE JOIST

HEADER

2. Fitting in the headers.

◆ Install two double-joist hangers on each double joist at the planned locations of the headers.

◆ From lumber the same size as the joists, cut two pairs of boards to serve as headers between the double joists. Nail each pair together with three 3-inch galvanized common nails spaced every 16 inches.

◆ Lift each header into place *(left)* and fasten it to the joist hangers at each end.

3. Filling in with cripple joists.

◆ Measuring from one of the single joists, mark the locations of the cripple joists on the rim joist and headers, spacing them the same distance apart as regular joists. Install joist hangers at these locations on the headers.

◆ Cut cripple joists to fit between the ledger and the first header, fit each one in place, and fasten it at both ends to the joist hangers with galvanized framing-anchor nails.

◆ Cut cripple joists to fit between the other header and rim joist. Fit each one in place and fasten it at one end to the joist hanger with galvanized framing-anchor nails and at the other end to the rim joist with three $3\frac{1}{2}$-inch galvanized spiral-shank nails *(right)*.

HEADER

RIM JOIST

CRIPPLE JOIST

4. Adding corner braces.

◆ From joist lumber, cut four corner braces to fit between the headers and double joists, beveling both ends at 45 degrees.

◆ Fit one brace into place and fasten it to the frame at each end with three nails. Fasten the remaining corner braces in the same way *(right)*.

FRAMING A WINDOW WELL

To prevent a deck from blocking light to a basement window, you can frame an opening around the window. To do so, attach the ledger to the wall in two sections, one on each side of the window. Frame the opening with double joists—located at the standard joist spacings—and a header at the desired distance from the window. In the example shown here, the double joist to the left of the window has one length of lumber cut $1\frac{1}{2}$ inches longer than the other so that it can be nailed to the end of the ledger next to the window; the other length is secured to the ledger with a multipurpose framing anchor. Because the joist spacing is standard, the double joist on the right side is several inches past the opening, requiring a cripple joist to be fastened to the end of the ledger and to the header.

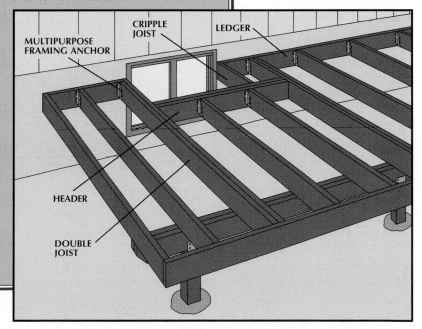

Adding one or more deck levels can smooth the transition between the yard and house, or add interest to an otherwise ordinary design. Distinct levels can also be used to define areas for specific activities, such as dining or sun bathing.

A Platform: The simplest way to add a level is to build a platform and fasten it on top of the joists of the main deck *(below and opposite)*. Since this design uses more lumber than most other methods, it is best for platforms of modest size, such as a landing in front of a door or a step between two deck levels.

A Lower Level: A second deck can be hung from the front of the main deck to allow one or more steps between levels *(page 54)*. Alternatively, place the lower level at the side of the deck by using a split beam attached to the posts of the main deck *(pages 54-55)*.

Steps Between Levels: To link levels, you can make the transition with one or more stacked platforms *(page 55)*. Plan the drop between the levels to be an even multiple of the height of the platforms. When made of 2-by-6 lumber, each step will be 7 inches high if you are using 2-by-4 decking, $6\frac{3}{4}$ inches high with 5/4 decking. Lay decking *(pages 62-68)* on the main deck before you install the platforms so the bottom step will be the correct height.

To make a transition from a low-level deck to the ground, build one or more steps the length of the deck *(pages 56-57)*. For the steps to be the correct height, plan the height of the deck when you are laying the foundation *(pages 28-29)* so that the vertical rise of each step will be no higher than about 7 inches when the deck boards are in place. Otherwise, you may need to rip boards to keep the rise of the steps equal.

TOOLS

Tape measure
Combination
  square
Mason's line
Chalk line

Circular saw
Maul
Hammer
Electric drill
Wrenches
Post-hole digger
Concrete tools

MATERIALS

2 x 2s
Materials for casting
  footings and
  setting posts
Pressure-treated
  lumber for ledgers,
  posts, beams, joists,
  and other framing
Post caps
Multipurpose
  framing anchors

Joist hangers
Framing-anchor
  nails
Galvanized lag
  screws ($\frac{3}{8}$" x 4")
  and washers
Galvanized carriage
  bolts ($\frac{1}{2}$" x 6", 7")
  and washers
Galvanized spiral-
  shank nails ($3\frac{1}{2}$")
Galvanized common
  nails (3")

SAFETY TIPS

Goggles protect your eyes when you are using a power tool or hammering.

ADDING A PLATFORM

1. Assembling the platform.
◆ Assemble a frame of the desired size from four pieces of 2-by-6 lumber, butting them together or beveling the corners. Fasten the corners with $3\frac{1}{2}$-inch galvanized spiral-shank nails.
◆ Fill in the frame with joists spaced the same distance apart as the deck joists, nailing them to the sides of the frame so they will run at right angles to the house.
◆ If the house has flat siding, install spacers along the wall *(page 25)* where the platform will rest. For overlapping siding, remove a section the length of the platform *(page 26)*.
◆ Position the frame on top of the main deck *(right)*, setting one of the sides flush against the wall.

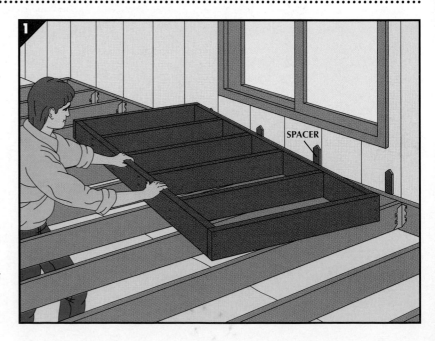

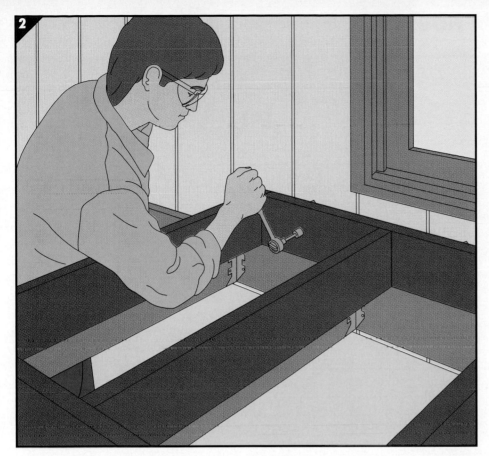

2. Fastening the platform.

◆ Fasten the back of the platform to the house wall through the spacers with galvanized $\frac{3}{8}$- by 4-inch lag screws and washers *(left)* as for a ledger *(pages 25-26)*.

◆ Toenail the front of the platform to each joist that it crosses with a $3\frac{1}{2}$-inch galvanized spiral-shank nail.

3. Adding a support joist.

When the platform extends past a joist at either end and leaves more than 4 inches of space between it and the next joist, add a short joist to support the decking up against the platform at that end.

◆ Cut a piece of joist lumber to fit as blocking between the joists.

◆ Place the blocking a few inches beyond the front edge of the platform between the joists straddled by the end of the platform, then nail the blocking to the joists.

◆ With galvanized framing-anchor nails, fasten a joist hanger to the deck ledger about 4 inches beyond the edge of the platform.

◆ Cut a support joist long enough to fit between the deck ledger and the blocking, then fasten it to the joist hanger with framing-anchor nails and to the blocking with three spiral-shank nails *(right)*.

◆ If necessary, install a support joist on the opposite side of the platform.

LEDGER

SUPPORT JOIST

BLOCKING

STEPPING DOWN FROM HOUSE LEVEL

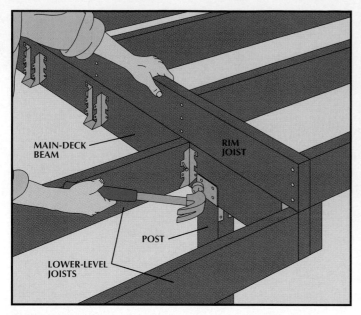

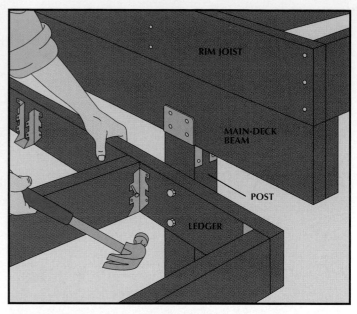

One step down.

◆ Build the main deck *(pages 20-51)*, but align the outer edges of the beam and rim joist.

◆ For a single step down, set posts and beam for the far end of the lower level, using the beam on the main deck as a ledger for the lower deck.

◆ Install end joists for the lower deck, fastening the attached ends to the outer face of the main-deck beam. Use multipurpose framing anchors and rest the opposite ends on the lower-level beam.

◆ Attach joist hangers to the outer face of the main-deck beam *(pages 37-38)*, then add the remaining joists *(above)* and complete the lower-level frame *(page 39)*.

Two or three steps down.

◆ Build the main deck in the same manner as for a one-step level change *(left)*, then mark the vertical drop on the main-deck posts, measuring from the top edge of the rim joist.

◆ Position a ledger board across the posts so its top edge is level with the marks.

◆ Drill holes through the ledger and posts, and fasten the ledger to each post with two $\frac{1}{2}$- by 6-inch galvanized carriage bolts and washers.

◆ Attach the joists to the ledger *(above)* and complete the lower-level frame *(page 39)*.

◆ Add one or more transition steps *(opposite)*.

SIDE-BY-SIDE DECKS

1. Attaching the beam.

◆ Build the upper deck *(pages 20-51)*, then lay out the lower deck and set its posts, counting the last post of the upper level as the first post of the lower one.

◆ At the house wall, mark the top of the lower ledger, measuring from the upper ledger a distance equal to the planned vertical drop between the decks.

◆ Install a ledger for the lower level at the mark, spacing it as shown in the inset so the end joists of the two decks will lie alongside each other.

◆ Tack a split beam between the posts *(page 34)* of the lower deck.

◆ Drill holes for two $\frac{1}{2}$- by 7-inch galvanized carriage bolts through the beam into each post *(right)* and tighten the bolts.

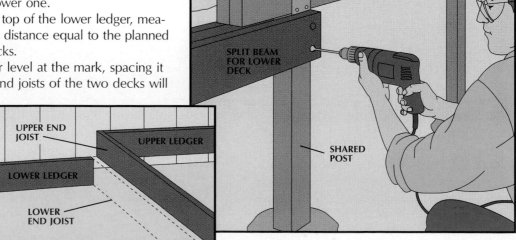

2. Adding joists.
◆ Install an end joist for the lower deck, positioning it alongside, but not under, the end joist of the upper deck *(left)*.
◆ Fasten the remaining joists *(pages 37-39)*.

UPPER END JOIST

LOWER END JOIST

SPLIT BEAM

A TRANSITION STEP

Installing the platform.
◆ Build a two-level deck and install the decking *(pages 62-68)* on the lower level.
◆ Construct a platform *(page 52, Step 1)*, place it on the lower deck, and fasten it to the beam or posts of the upper deck with $\frac{3}{8}$- by 4-inch galvanized lag screws and washers.
◆ Toenail each joist of the platform to the decking with $3\frac{1}{2}$-inch galvanized spiral-shank nails spaced every 16 inches *(right)*.

PLATFORM

1. Positioning the face board.

◆ Frame a low-level deck *(page 40)*, planning its finished height so that each step will be about 7 inches high when the decking is in place.

◆ Run a string line parallel to and $11\frac{1}{4}$ inches from the rim joist—with this distance, the step will be two deck boards in width—and mark locations for piers at least every 10 feet along it.

◆ Cast piers at the marks as described on page 28,

Step 1, but set the tops of the tubes at ground level instead of 2 inches above it and level them by raising any that are too low.

◆ From 2-by-6 lumber, cut a face board the length of the deck.

◆ Set the face board on the piers parallel to the rim joist and measure at several points to position its outer face $11\frac{1}{4}$ inches from the rim joist *(above)*.

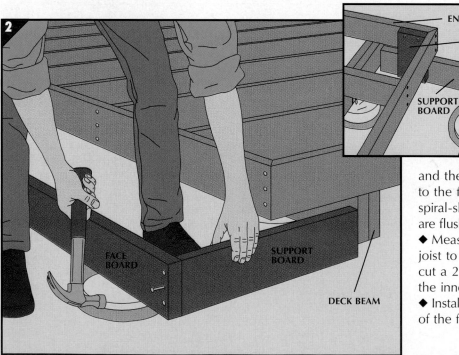

2. Installing face-board end supports.

◆ Measure the distance between the face board and the deck beam, then cut two 2-by-6s to this length as end supports.

◆ Holding a support board level between the face board and the beam at one end of the deck, fasten it to the face board with three $3\frac{1}{2}$-inch galvanized spiral-shank nails so the top edges of the pieces are flush *(left)*, then toenail the board to the beam.

◆ Measure from the top edge of the deck's end joist to the bottom edge of the support board, cut a 2-by-6 cleat to this length, and fasten it to the inner faces of the boards *(inset)*.

◆ Install the other end support at the opposite end of the face board in the same way.

3. Adding support boards.

◆ For every second deck joist, cut a support board to the same length as the end supports.

◆ Fasten each board to the beam and face board as in Step 2, aligning the piece with a deck joist *(left)*.

FACE BOARD   SUPPORT BOARDS

WRAPAROUND STEPS

If you want to build a transition step all the way around a deck *(photograph)*, support the section that runs along the rim joist as shown opposite and above, but cast an additional pier where the face boards of both steps meet at the corner; bevel the ends of the face boards at 45 degrees. To support the step that parallels the deck joists, hang wood cleats from the end joist *(opposite, Step 2 inset)*, then butt the support boards against the cleats and fasten them with nails. For a drop that exceeds one step, you can erect a series of steps by building the bottom step in the same manner as the platform described on page 55, then stacking the steps on top of it.

Adding a hot tub to a deck can increase your enjoyment of the outdoor living area. You can make the tub the centerpiece of the deck, or you can design a special area or add another level in order to accommodate the unit.

The easiest type of hot tub to install is a portable unit. Completely self-contained, such a model requires no special plumbing. After the tub is set into place in the deck, it is filled with water from a garden hose and plugged into an appropriate outdoor electrical outlet *(opposite).*

Supporting a Hot Tub: Portable units are generally about 3 to 4 feet high. For a customized appearance, you can mount the tub flush with the surface of the deck. To do so, you will need to frame an opening in the deck and build a concrete or wooden platform to support the tub. To keep the tub as low as possible, you can support it on a concrete slab cast slightly above ground level. Excavate 6 inches below the surface and lay a 4-inch bed of gravel, then cast a level 4-inch slab. For a taller deck, you will need to frame a platform under the tub *(below).* The structural requirements will vary depending on the weight of the unit and soil conditions; have the local building department review your plans before you start.

Accessing the Controls: You may want to hide the hot-tub support by adding a skirt around the deck *(pages 120-125).* Most portable models have controls or equipment that must be accessed on occasion from the side, so include a door or hinged panel in the skirt.

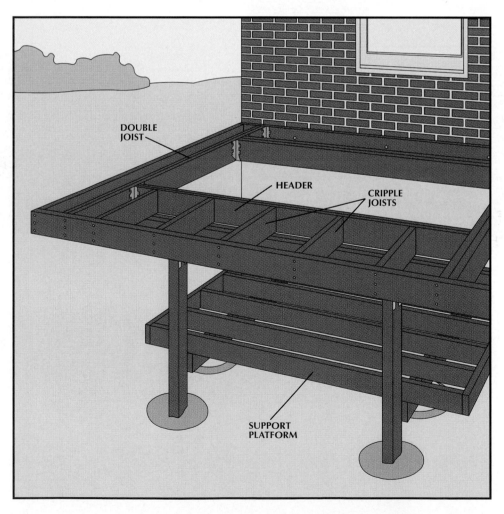

DOUBLE JOIST

HEADER

CRIPPLE JOISTS

SUPPORT PLATFORM

Framing for a hot tub on a support deck.

The hot tub at left is supported on a low wooden platform framed much like a freestanding deck *(page 40)*; however, the footings may need to be slightly larger—often 18 inches in diameter—depending on local codes. In addition, the joists are typically spaced 1 foot apart to support the weight of the unit. The height of the platform will depend on how much of the tub you wish to leave exposed above the main deck.

In this design, the upper deck is framed around the tub with double joists, headers, and cripple joists as described on pages 49 to 51. The opening is about 4 inches larger all around than the unit to allow for the overhang of the decking plus a slight gap. If the tub is round or octagonal, you will need corner braces to support the ends of the deck boards *(page 51)*. Once the unit is in place, you can scribe the boards to match its contours *(page 71)*.

A portable hot tub must be plugged into a nearby outdoor outlet equipped with a ground-fault circuit interrupter (GFCI). Usually, this outlet is wired to a dedicated 20-amp grounded circuit run from the house service panel to the tub; however, the wiring restrictions may vary depending on the tub model and on local codes. Most codes require that the outlet for the tub be located within sight of the tub's access panel. If the panel is under the deck, as in a flush-mounted unit, code may require a second GFCI outlet above the deck for powering radios or other electrical devices.

To run the wiring for a flush-mounted hot tub *(right)*, drill a hole for underground feeder (UF) cable through the house's band joist and the deck ledger. Fish the cable from the service panel through the hole and run it along a deck joist to the outlet location, fastening it with cable clamps at the house and the outlet, and at a minimum of every $4\frac{1}{2}$ feet in between. Attach the cable to the outlet box with a weatherproof connector, then fasten the box to the joist. To wire the GFCI outlet *(inset)*, attach the cable's black wire to the brass terminal labeled "LINE" and the white wire to the silver terminal marked "LINE". Fasten a green jumper wire to the receptacle's ground screw and another to the ground screw of the box, then join the jumpers and the copper wire of the UF cable with a wire cap. Next, drill a hole through the decking and bring a second cable up through it from the service panel. Install a second GFCI outlet on the house wall, protecting the exposed cable with electrical conduit. Finally, seal the hole in the house wall with caulk.

Once the receptacles and the hot tub have been installed, have a licensed electrician complete the installation by hooking up the new circuits to the service panel; bonding the tub to any permanent metal objects within 10 feet of it—such as gutters or fences; and running a separate ground wire from the tub to the service panel if the manufacturer requires it.

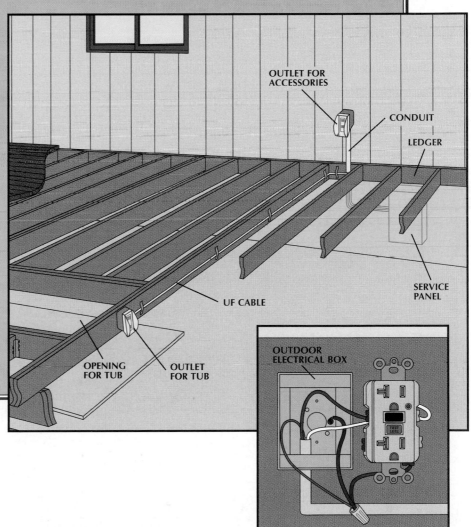

OUTLET FOR ACCESSORIES

CONDUIT

LEDGER

SERVICE PANEL

UF CABLE

OPENING FOR TUB

OUTLET FOR TUB

OUTDOOR ELECTRICAL BOX

3

Decking, Railings, and Stairs

Once the deck structure is framed, you can put down the deck boards, and add railings and stairs. Decking and railings can define or complement the style of the deck, while the placement and size of stairs establishes traffic patterns. Finally, you can coat the deck boards and details with a protective finish to increase their resistance to wear and tear.

Building deck stairs →

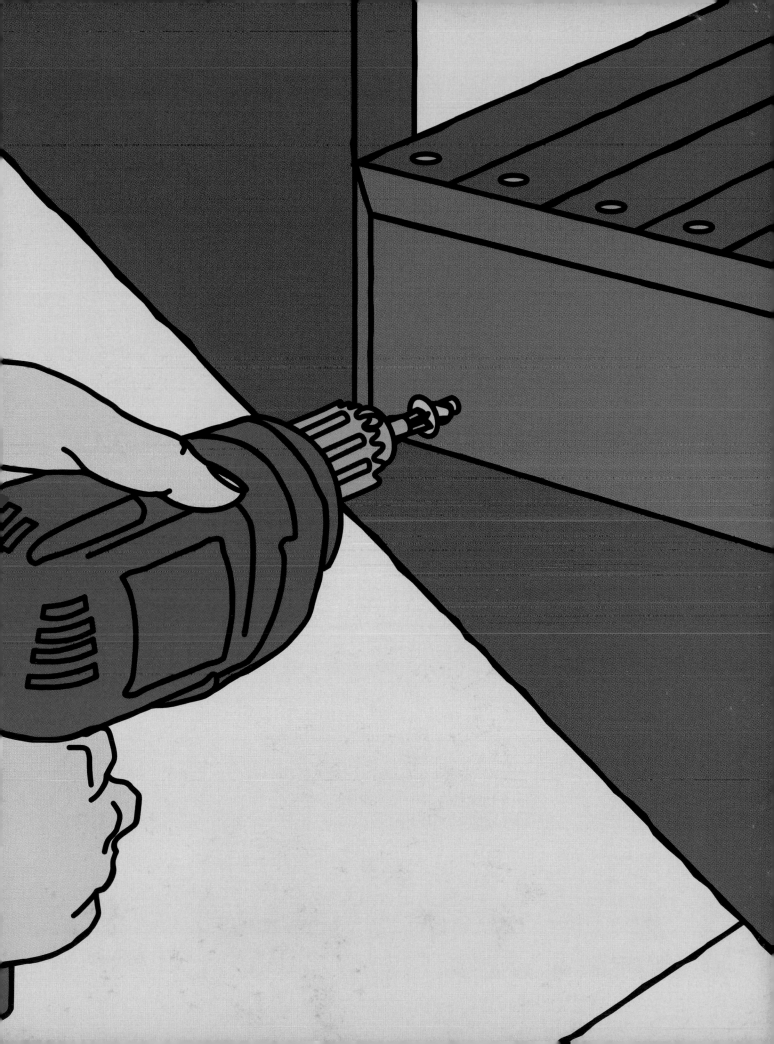

The decking pattern is an important element in the style of the deck. The simplest design is to run the boards perpendicular to the joists; you can modify this style by combining boards of various widths. Other alternatives are to lay the decking diagonally across the joists or add a picture frame *(pages 67-68)*—but avoid busy patterns, particularly on a small structure. For a wraparound deck *(pages 45-48)*, miter the ends that meet at the corner *(page 66)*. Decking at an angled corner *(pages 42-44)* can follow the line of the angle, or be cut on a curve *(pages 69-70)*. When you have built a frame around an obstacle *(pages 49-51)*, you can scribe the decking to fit closely around the object *(page 71)*.

Fastening Decking: Decking can be anchored to the framing with galvanized screws or nails. Another option is to fasten the boards with invisible clips *(pages 64-65)*. Nails are fast to drive, but likely to work loose over time—to minimize popping of nails, use the spiral-shank variety. Renting a pneumatic nailer will speed the work, but if you plan to drive the nails by hand, recess the heads with a nail set.

If you will be adding an overhead *(pages 112-115)*, omit the end boards until the overhead is built.

Finishing Touches: After the decking is laid down, you can trim it flush with the edges of the deck's framing or leave a 1-inch overhang. For a flush installation, hide the ends of the boards with a fascia *(page 64)* or add a cap installed after the railing posts are in place *(page 87, box)*. If you are using redwood or cedar decking, you can make the fascia of the same wood to hide the rougher framing lumber. If you do not plan to cap the decking, round over exposed edges with a router to prevent chipping, being sure to stay clear of the fasteners.

A trap door is a handy feature *(pages 72-73)* that allows access to items stored or located under the deck such as outdoor faucets.

 TOOLS

Electric drill
Chalk line
Circular saw   Combination
Saber saw   square
Handsaw   Hand plane
Hammer   Wood chisel
Pry bar   Mallet

 **MATERIALS**

Decking and fascia
   lumber
Pressure-treated 2 x 2s
   and blocking
Plywood scraps ($\frac{1}{8}$", $\frac{1}{4}$")

Galvanized spiral-shank
   nails (3", $3\frac{1}{2}$")
Invisible deck clips
Framing-anchor nails
Deck screws ($2\frac{1}{2}$")
Butt hinges
Recessed drawer pull

 SAFETY TIPS

Protect your eyes with goggles when using a power saw or hammering. Don a dust mask to cut pressure-treated wood and wash thoroughly after handling the lumber.

A BASIC PATTERN

Fastening boards.

◆ Cut a straight board to the deck's finished length—or plan a splice *(opposite)*—and place it along the house, offsetting it from the wall with spacers of $\frac{1}{8}$-inch plywood.

◆ Fasten the board to each joist with two $3\frac{1}{2}$-inch galvanized spiral-shank nails.

◆ Continue with boards a few inches longer than the deck, positioning them with plywood spacers and leaving an overhang at both ends. To fasten a bowed board, place its convex edge along the previous board and have a helper pry the end into line while you nail it *(right)*.

◆ Lay the decking until you are a few boards from the edge of the deck; then, measure the remaining space. If the boards won't fit without ripping them, cut the last two or three equally or finish with a wider board, rather than end with one very narrow board.

◆ At each end of the deck, snap a chalk line across the decking, fasten a straight board as a saw guide *(page 66, Step 1)*, and trim the ends of the decking with a circular saw.

SPACER

Decking Spacers

An alternative to using pieces of $\frac{1}{8}$-inch ply-wood to keep deck boards apart as you install them is to make spacers out of nails and small wood blocks. Simply drive a $3\frac{1}{2}$-inch nail partway through each block and slip the nail between decking boards so the block sits on the surface *(right)*.

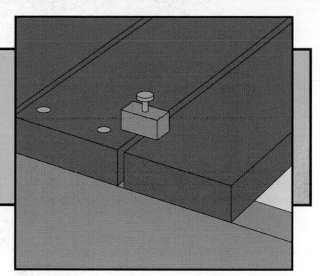

Splicing boards.

◆ For boards that are too short to span the deck's entire length, lay them end-to-end and locate the joint over a joist.

◆ Place a spacer between the spliced boards and the adjacent board, then butt the board ends tightly together.

◆ Drill two pilot holes at an angle through each board and into the joist under the splice.

◆ Drive a nail into each hole *(left)*. If you will be making several splices, locate them over different joists so the joint lines are staggered.

A DECK WRENCH

If you are laying decking without a helper, the tool in the photograph at right will help you straighten bowed boards. The jaw of the tool fits over the joist and the cam lies along the decking; pulling on the handle straightens the board and locks the tool in position while you nail the board in place.

ADDING A FASCIA

Trimming the deck.
◆ Cut three lengths of 5/4 stock to fit as fascia boards around the perimeter of the deck—four pieces for a free-standing deck—beveling the ends to meet at the corners.
◆ Fasten the boards to the end and rim joists so the upper edges are flush with the surface of the decking, driving five 3-inch galvanized spiral-shank nails at each corner *(right)* and two more nails every 2 feet in between.
◆ Round the beveled corners slightly with a hand plane.

FASCIA BOARD

USING INVISIBLE FASTENERS

1. Fastening the first board.
◆ Fasten a straight board along the wall of the house as for an installation with nails *(page 62)*, but drive only one nail through the face of the board into each joist as close to the wall as possible.
◆ Drive a second nail at an angle through the outer edge of the board into each joist *(left)*.

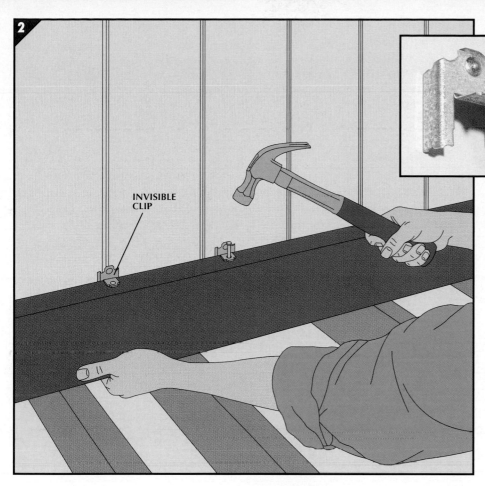

INVISIBLE CLIP

2. Attaching the clips.
◆ Lay the second board on edge across the joists.
◆ Place an invisible clip *(photograph)* on the edge of the board about 2 inches from an end joist and tap the clip with a hammer, driving the teeth into the wood.
◆ Fasten the clip to the board with a galvanized framing-anchor nail.
◆ Secure a clip to the board for every joist, offset about 2 inches from the joist location *(left)*.

3. Installing the boards.
◆ Lay the board flat so the clips sit a few inches from the first board, offsetting them from the joists.
◆ Place a wood block against the outer edge of the second board near one end and tap the block with a hammer *(right)* to drive the boards together and force the clips under the first board. Work along the length of the board until the entire edge is snug against the first.
◆ Nail the outer edge of the second board to the joists as you did for the first board.
◆ Install the remaining boards in the same way, then trim their ends.

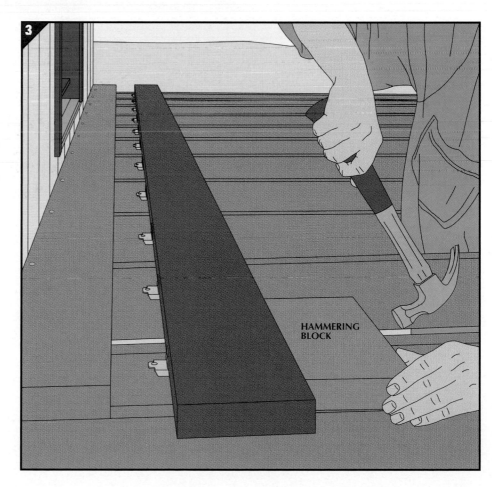

HAMMERING BLOCK

DECKING THAT MEETS AT A CORNER

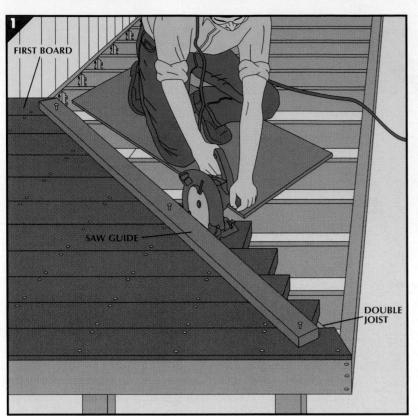

FIRST BOARD

SAW GUIDE

DOUBLE JOIST

1. Decking the first section.
On a wraparound-deck frame *(pages 45-48)*, the decking is mitered to meet over the double joist at the corner.

◆ Fasten the first board of one of the sections *(page 62)*, cutting one end flush with the end joist and mitering the other to align with the middle of the double joist.

◆ Finish laying the decking on the first section, spacing the boards $\frac{1}{8}$ inch apart and splicing short ones end-to-end *(page 63)* so each board overlaps the double joist. Avoid driving any nails along or beyond the seam in the double joist.

◆ Tack a straight board to the decking as a saw guide, positioning it so the saw will trim the boards in line with the joint in the double joist.

◆ Working on a sheet of plywood, miter the ends of the deck boards *(left)*.

2. Decking the second section.
◆ Position the first board of the second section *(right)* and fasten it as described in Step 1, butting its end against the end of its counterpart in the first section of the deck.

◆ Miter one end of each remaining board, then nail them down, butting the ends between the two sections along the corner double joist.

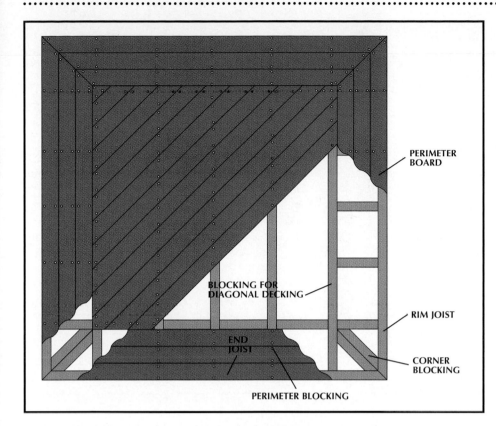

PERIMETER BOARD

BLOCKING FOR DIAGONAL DECKING

RIM JOIST

END JOIST

CORNER BLOCKING

PERIMETER BLOCKING

Diagonal decking with a frame.

On the deck at left, a center section of decking laid diagonally is framed by perimeter boards meeting at mitered corners. On an attached deck, you can omit the perimeter boards along the house.

To support this pattern of decking, the understructure must have end joists spaced 16 inches center-to-center from the adjacent joists. For 2-by-6 deck boards, the intermediate joists are laid at 16-inch intervals; 12 inch-intervals for 5/4 decking. Parallel to the rim joists and 16 inches inside them, blocking supports the ends of the diagonal deck boards. Blocking is also installed along the end joists to hold up the perimeter boards. Corner blocking is fashioned in a similar manner as the corner joist on a wraparound deck *(page 47)*.

END JOIST

BLOCKING

PERIMETER BLOCKING

PERIMETER BLOCKING

JOIST

CORNER BLOCKING

RIM JOIST

1. Adding the blocking.

◆ Build a deck frame *(pages 20-40)*, spacing the joists as described above.

◆ For every 16 inches of end-joist length, cut a piece of joist lumber to fit as perimeter blocking between each end joist and the adjacent joist. Install the blocking at 16-inch intervals, driving three $3\frac{1}{2}$-inch galvanized spiral-shank nails per end.

◆ Cut blocking for the diagonal decking to fit between each pair of intermediate joists 16 inches from the rim joists

and fasten each piece in place, face-nailing one end and toenailing the other *(above, left)*.

◆ At each corner of the deck, measure the distance between the angles formed by the end and rim joists, and by the first piece of perimeter blocking and the first intermediate joist. Cut two lengths of blocking to length, beveling both ends of each piece. Fasten the blocks together so they form points at both ends, then slip the corner blocking into place *(above, right)*, and fasten each end with three nails.

2. Laying the diagonal boards.

◆ Set a short board diagonally across the joists, aligning its outer edge with the inner tip of the corner blocking. With a combination square, angle the board at 45 degrees to the joists.

◆ Fasten the board with two nails to the blocking and the first intermediate joist; avoid driving a nail near the outer face of the joist—you will be trimming the decking along the joist later.

◆ Continue laying decking diagonally, using boards long enough to overhang the first intermediate joist and the blocking *(right)* and spacing the boards $\frac{1}{8}$ inch apart. Fasten them to the joist and blocking.

◆ When you are a few boards away from the opposite corner, rip the last pieces to width as needed to align them with the tip of the corner blocking.

◆ Trim the decking *(page 66, Step 1)* in line with the outer sides of the blocking and the first intermediate joists.

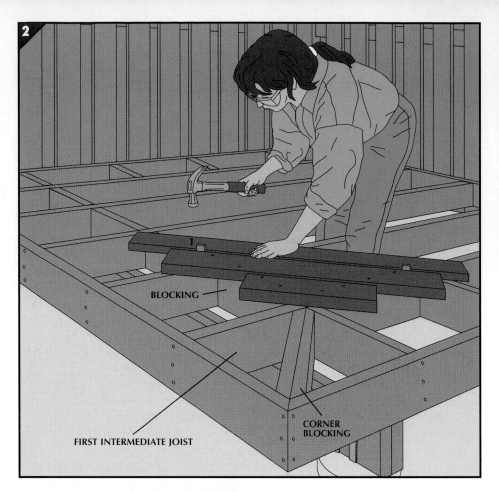

BLOCKING

FIRST INTERMEDIATE JOIST

CORNER BLOCKING

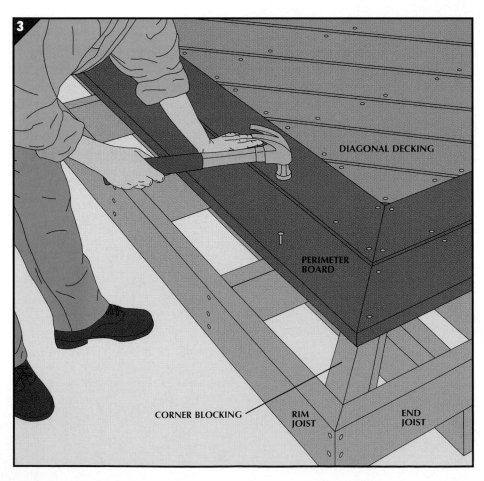

DIAGONAL DECKING

PERIMETER BOARD

CORNER BLOCKING

RIM JOIST

END JOIST

3. Laying the perimeter boards.

◆ Cut four lengths of deck boards to fit around the perimeter of the diagonal decking, mitering the ends at 45 degrees so the joints will align with the corners. If you want the last boards to sit flush with the outer sides of the end and rim joists rather than overhang them by $\frac{3}{4}$ inch, trim $\frac{1}{4}$ inch from the width of each piece.

◆ Set one of the perimeter boards in place, aligning its ends with the joints in the corner blocking and butting it against the diagonal decking.

◆ Fasten the board to every joist and length of blocking it crosses; nail the ends to the corner blocking.

◆ Install the three remaining boards, butting the mitered ends together.

◆ Lay two more rows of perimeter decking in the same way *(left)*.

CUTTING A CURVE

A deck with rounded corners.
A deck with curved corners is built on a frame with angled corners *(pages 42-44)*. Cut long enough to overhang the end and angled rim joists, the deck boards are then trimmed straight along the end joist and in a curve along the angled joist.

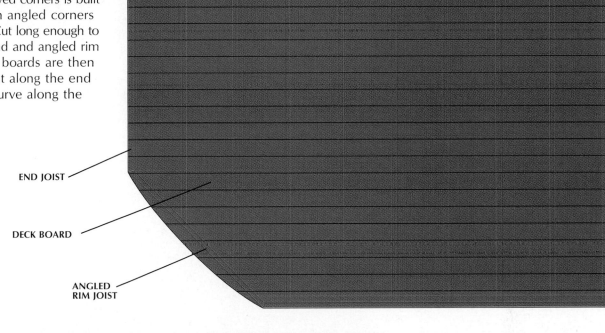

END JOIST

DECK BOARD

ANGLED
RIM JOIST

ANGLED
RIM JOIST

1. Drawing the curve.
◆ Frame a deck with an angled corner *(pages 42-44)* for each corner you wish to curve.
◆ Lay the deck boards *(pages 62-63)* so they overhang the end joist and the angled rim joist by a few inches.
◆ Drive a nail partway into the decking directly above each outside end of the angled rim.
◆ Set a length of $\frac{1}{4}$-inch plywood a foot or two longer than the distance between the nails on edge so one side is against the nails and trace a straight line along the molding.
◆ Pull back on the plywood so the middle is about $2\frac{1}{2}$ inches behind the marked line, then trace a curved line along the piece *(left)*.

2. Cutting the decking.

◆ Trim the ends of the deck boards flush with the outer face of the end joist.

◆ Cut along the curved line with a saber saw *(right)*.

A DECK WITH MULTIPLE CURVES

The ground-level deck in the photograph at right is built with a series of curves that help the deck blend into its setting. The structure is built with angled corners *(pages 42-44)* and the deck boards cut on a curve. To lay out such curves, you can use a garden hose, filled with water to keep it from kinking, and pin it in place with a nail driven to one side at the ends of each curve. Trace the curves on the decking and trim the boards with a saber saw, as described above. The decking can over- hang the understructure by a maximum of 4 inches. This deck features a fascia *(page 64)* made of flexible benderboard.

FITTING AROUND AN OBSTACLE

1. Laying the decking.
◆ Fasten the decking, starting at the house wall *(pages 62-63)*.
◆ As you lay the decking around the obstacle, trim the boards to size and cut notches so you can place them within a few inches of the obstruction *(left)*—if the obstacle is a tree, leave a space of about 5 inches around it so it has room to grow.

NOTCH

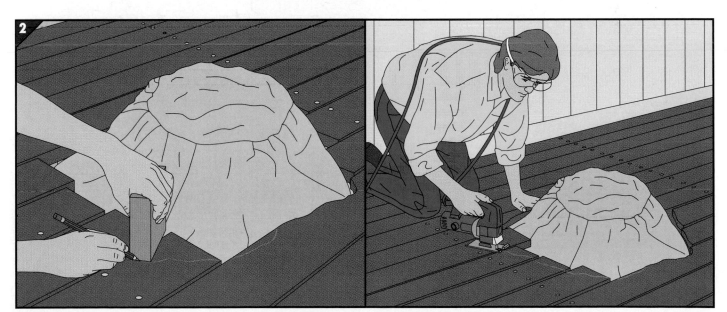

2. Cutting the decking around the obstruction.
◆ Set a 2-by-4 block on the decking—use a 2-by-6 if the obstruction is a tree—with an edge against the obstacle and mark a line along the opposite edge, following the perimeter of the obstruction with the block and pencil *(above, left)* until you have scribed a line around it.
◆ With a saber saw, cut into the end of a board to the scribed line, then continue sawing along the line *(above, right)*.

BUILDING A TRAP DOOR

1. Cutting the decking.

◆ Outline the door on the decking between two joists, aligning the marks with the joists' inner faces and making the outline no longer than the width of four deck boards.

◆ Cut along the lines with a circular saw, starting with a technique known as a plunge cut: Hold the saw with only the front of the base plate on the decking and the blade clear of the surface. Retract the blade guard with the lever, align the blade with one of the marks near one end, turn on the saw and slowly lower the blade into the wood until the base plate is flat, then advance the saw to the opposite end of the line *(right)*.

◆ Saw along the other line in the same way, then complete the ends of the cuts with a handsaw.

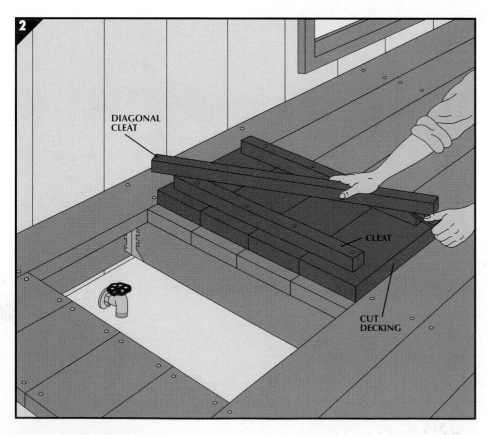

DIAGONAL CLEAT

CLEAT

CUT DECKING

2. Making the door.

◆ Place the cut boards alongside the opening, ends aligned, lining up their edges with the decking below.

◆ Cut two 2-by-2 cleats 2 inches shorter than the combined width of the cut boards. Position the cleats 2 inches in from the edges, centered across the width and leaving 1 inch on each end, then fasten them to each board with a $2\frac{1}{2}$-inch coated deck screw.

◆ Measure the diagonal between the cleats, then cut a third cleat a few inches longer than the distance. Place it across the cleats, aligning its edges with the corners, and mark its underside along the inner edges of the cleats *(left)*.

◆ Trim the diagonal cleat to length and fasten it to the deck boards so the cut ends butt against the straight cleats.

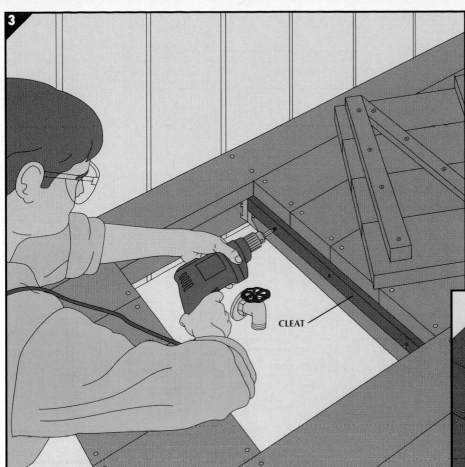

3. Preparing the opening.

◆ Cut two 2-by-2 cleats to the same length as the opening and fasten one to a joist adjoining the opening, flush with the top edge, with 2½-inch deck screws spaced every 8 inches (left).

◆ Fasten the second cleat to the other joist in the same way.

If you want to use the space as a storage compartment, drill pilot holes for two galvanized hooks into each joist just below the cleats and twist a hook into each hole, then hang a plastic-coated wire basket of the right size on the hooks (inset).

4. Hinging the door.

◆ Place the door in the opening, setting it on the cleats, and position two 3-inch galvanized butt hinges across the seam between the edge of the door nearest the house and the deck.

◆ Mark the screw holes, remove the hinges, drill a pilot hole for the screws provided at each mark, and screw in the hinges (right).

◆ Center a recessed drawer pull (photograph) on the door near the opposite end and outline its faceplate on the surface.

◆ With a wood chisel, cut a mortise within the outline equal in depth to the thickness of the faceplate, then fasten the pull in place with the screws provided.

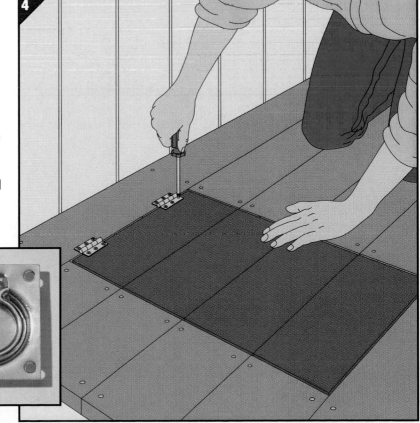

When a deck is more than three steps above ground level, you will need to build a flight of stairs if you want convenient access to the yard. You can also use stairs to link two deck levels. On a low-level deck, you may want to add a ramp for wheelchair access or for rolling heavy items onto the deck or into the house.

Design and Materials: The stairs on these pages are supported by three notched stringers *(pages 75-77)* made of 2-by-12s; choose lumber that is as straight and knot-free as possible. The stringers are attached to the end or rim joist and rest on a concrete slab—for a flight of more than three steps, the stringers are fastened to the slab as well.

The treads are typically made of the same lumber as the deck, but you can use boards of different widths for decorative effect. The risers can be enclosed *(page 78)* or left open, and the ends of the treads can overhang the stringers or be cut flush with them. If you choose to cut the treads flush, you can conceal the ends of the treads and risers with face boards, but to do so you will have to attach the stringers to the deck in a different way *(page 77, box).* For a more elaborate style of stairs, you can make the treads from 2-by-2s and hide the end grain *(pages 79-80).* Plan the proportions of the steps as described below.

Adding a Ramp: A ramp for a wheelchair requires a gradual slope—a rise of no more than 1 vertical inch for every horizontal foot. Because of the potential length of a straight ramp, it is practical only for low-level decks. To keep the structure from jutting out too far into the yard, build a landing at deck level and run the ramp along one side of the deck *(pages 81-82).* Make the ramp 42 inches wide and the landing 42 inches square.

 TOOLS

Carpenter's level (4')
Carpenter's square
Circular saw
Handsaw
Powdered chalk
Hammer
Electric drill
Pointed shovel
Concrete tools

 **MATERIALS**

Pressure-treated
  2 x 6s, 2 x 8s, 2 x
  12s, 1 x 8s, 4 x 4s
Pressure-treated
  5/4 stock
Materials for casting
  concrete piers
Wood shims
Post caps
Multipurpose framing
  anchors
Angle irons
Galvanized spiral-
  shank nails ($3\frac{1}{2}$")
Galvanized framing-
  anchor nails
Deck screws (1", $2\frac{1}{2}$")
Masonry screws ($1\frac{1}{2}$")

SAFETY TIPS

Put on goggles when using a power tool or hammering. Add a dust mask to cut pressure-treated wood and wash your hands thoroughly after handling it.

Stair dimensions.

While there is some flexibility in stair design, certain aspects of the construction are governed by building codes. The unit rise—measured from the surface of one step to the next—must fall between 6 and $7\frac{1}{2}$ inches. For your stairs, choose a figure that divides evenly into the total rise—the vertical distance between the deck surface and the slab at the bottom of the stairs. The unit run, measured from the face of one riser to the next, can be from 10 to 16 inches. Choose a figure that will accommodate the tread materials you plan to use without ripping boards; for closed-riser steps, allow for

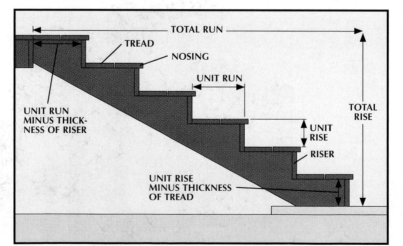

a slight nosing that extends past the front of each riser. For example, a $10\frac{1}{2}$-inch unit run will accommodate treads made of two 2-by-6s with a $\frac{1}{8}$-inch gap between them and a $\frac{5}{8}$-inch nosing. Since

there is no tread at the bottom of the stairs or riser at the top, you'll need to trim the thickness of a tread off the bottom of the stringers and the thickness of a riser off the back of the top of the stringers to make the top and bottom steps the same height and depth as the others. As you determine the rise and run for your project, keep in mind that steps with a shorter rise and deeper run are more comfortable to climb, but will extend farther from the deck. You can make the flight of stairs 36 to 48 inches wide.

TOTAL-RUN MARK

1. Measuring the total rise.

To determine the total rise of the stairs on ground that may slope, you need to measure the drop from the deck surface to the spot where the slab for the foot of the stairs will be placed.

◆ Measure the vertical distance between the deck surface and the ground, then divide the figure by an ideal unit rise of 7 inches. Round the result up to the next whole number to get the number of treads, then multiply this figure by the desired tread depth to determine the total run. Mark this distance with tape on a straight board.

◆ While a helper holds the board level on the deck with the tape at the edge, measure from the bottom edge of the board at the end to the ground to determine the total rise *(left)*. Make a chalk mark at this point.

◆ Adjust the unit rise to a figure that will divide evenly into this measurement.

2. Casting the slab.

◆ Make a chalk mark on the ground 15 inches in front of the one marked in Step 1 and another 15 inches behind it.

◆ Dig a hole 6 inches deep, about 1 foot wider than the stairs, between the second and third chalk marks. In poorly draining soil, make the hole 12 inches deep and lay a compacted 6-inch bed of gravel.

◆ Cut four 1-by-4s to fit around the inside of the hole as a form to contain the concrete you will pour. Nail the form together, then fasten two more 1-by-4s to the outer faces of the two longer pieces, flush with the top edges, to hold the form at the right height; slip shims under them, as needed, to level it *(right)*.

◆ Fill the form with concrete and, with a straight board, strike the surface flush with the top of the form. Smooth the concrete with a wood float and let the slab cure overnight.

FORM BOARDS

3. Cutting the stringers.

◆ With masking tape, mark the unit rise on the short arm of a carpenter's square and the unit run on the long arm.

◆ Set the square against a 2-by-12 so the tape marks are flush with the same edge of the boards. Mark the first unit run.

◆ Move the square along the 2-by-12 and mark the first unit rise and the next run *(right)*. Continue outlining the steps along the length of the board until you have marked the last unit run. Then, draw one additional rise.

◆ Square off the top and bottom of the layout.

◆ Draw a second line for the bottom of the stringer, subtracting the thickness of a tread. For closed-riser steps, make a second line for the top of the stringer, subtracting a riser's thickness *(inset)*.

◆ Cut the stringer with a circular saw, then finish the cuts with a handsaw.

◆ Use the first stringer as a template to lay out and cut out the other two.

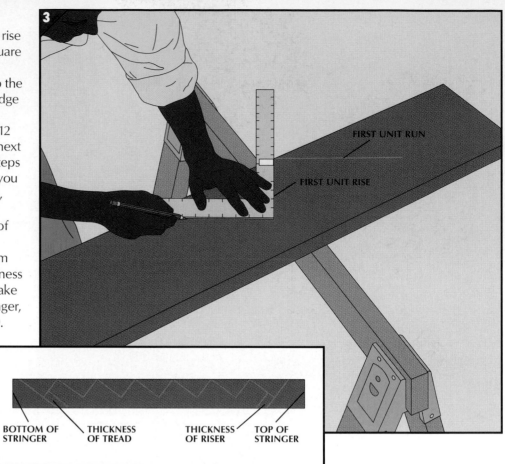

FIRST UNIT RUN

FIRST UNIT RISE

BOTTOM OF STRINGER   THICKNESS OF TREAD   THICKNESS OF RISER   TOP OF STRINGER

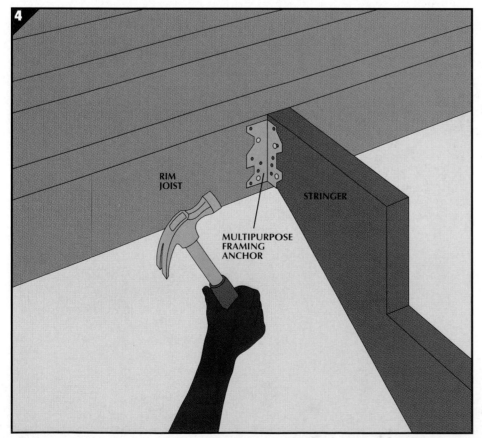

RIM JOIST

STRINGER

MULTIPURPOSE FRAMING ANCHOR

4. Fastening at the top.

◆ Draw three plumb lines on the edge of the deck's rim or end joist to indicate the tops of the stringers.

◆ Set an outer stringer in place against the deck so its top is flush with the top of the rim or end joist and the face is flush with the plumb line. Drive three $3\frac{1}{2}$-inch galvanized spiral-shank nails through the back of the joist into the end of the stringer.

◆ Fasten the inside face of the stringer to the deck with a multipurpose framing anchor and galvanized framing-anchor nails *(left)*.

◆ Fasten the remaining two stringers to the deck in the same way.

5. Anchoring to the slab.

◆ Adjust the bottom of the stringers so they are the same distance apart as at the top.

◆ Set an angle iron against the inside of one of the outer stringers and mark the screw holes on the concrete slab.

◆ Remove the angle iron and, with an electric drill and masonry bit, drill a pilot hole for a $1\frac{1}{2}$-inch masonry screw at each mark.

◆ Replace the angle iron and fasten it to the slab with masonry screws *(left)*, then fasten it to the stringer with 1-inch coated deck screws.

◆ Fasten the bottoms of the other two stringers in the same way.

ANGLE IRON

AN ALTERNATIVE STAIR ATTACHMENT

If you prefer the stairs to begin one step down from the deck, you can attach the stringers as shown below. Also use this method if you want to cover the ends of the treads and risers with face boards. Lay out the stringers as shown opposite, Step 3, but with one less riser since the rim or end joist will serve as the top riser. Splice a length of 2-by-6 blocking to the bottom of the rim or end joist, attaching it on the back with vertical cleats. Measure down one unit rise from the top of the end or rim joist to position the stringers and attach them with multipurpose framing anchors as shown opposite, Step 4. Then, cut the ends of two 2-by-12s at the same angle as the top and bottom of the stringers and fasten the face boards to the outer stringers every 8 inches with galvanized spiral-shank nails.

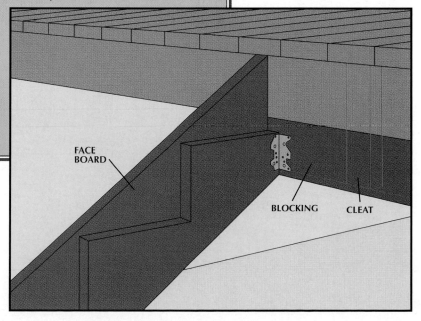

FACE BOARD

BLOCKING   CLEAT

CLOSING THE RISERS AND ADDING TREADS

RISER

1. Installing risers.
◆ Measure the distance between the outside faces of the two outer stringers at the bottom of the stairs and cut a 2-by-8 to length. Rip the board to the height of the first vertical section of the stringers.
◆ Set the riser against the stringers and fasten it to each stringer with three $2\frac{1}{2}$-inch coated deck screws.
◆ Cut the remaining risers, ripping them to match the unit rise, and install them in the same way *(left)*.

2. Adding the treads.
◆ For each unit run, cut a tread to the same length as the risers—here, each tread is made of two 2-by-6s.
◆ Starting at the bottom step, set the first 2-by-6 in place across the stringers against the riser and fasten it to each stringer with three screws.
◆ Attach the second board in the same way about $\frac{1}{8}$ inch from the first.
◆ Install the remaining treads *(right)*.

$\frac{1}{8}$" GAP

TREAD

1. Fastening the 2-by-2s.

◆ Make each tread by cutting seven 2-by-2s to a length equal to the distance between the outside faces of the two outer stringers.

◆ Set the 2-by-2s on the bottom step of the stringers, placing them so they are evenly spaced and the front piece is flush with the front of the stringers.

◆ Drill a pilot hole for a $2\frac{1}{2}$-inch coated deck screw where each 2-by-2 crosses a stringer *(left)*, then drive the screws.

TRICKS OF THE TRADE

Cutting 2-by-2s Quickly

To quickly cut 2-by-2s for stair treads to exactly the same length, cut them in groups. Align one end of the 2-by-2s and clamp them together with two bar clamps. With a carpenter's square, mark a line across the 2-by-2s at the desired length. Then, cut them all at once with a circular saw *(right)*.

2. Framing the treads.

◆ Beginning with the second tread, cut three pieces of 5/4 stock to wrap around the front and sides of the tread, beveling both ends of the front piece and the front end of the side pieces at 45 degrees; bevel the back end of the side pieces at 60 degrees.

◆ Attach a side piece to one of the stringers with two screws near each end so the top edge is flush with the surface of the tread. Then, fasten the front piece to each stringer with two screws. Finally, add the other end piece *(right)*.

◆ Round the beveled frame corners slightly with a hand plane.

◆ Frame the remaining steps in the same way, omitting the top and bottom steps. Once the stair-railing posts have been installed *(page 91)*, frame the top and bottom steps, cutting the end pieces to fit around the posts.

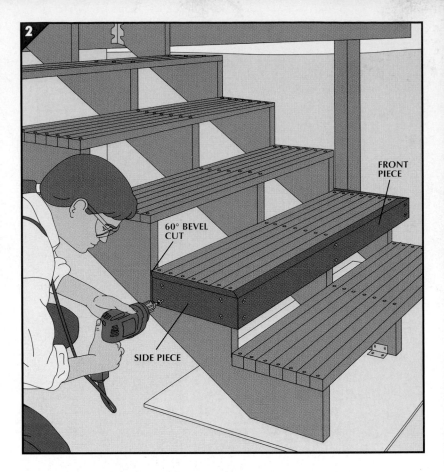

FRONT PIECE

60° BEVEL CUT

SIDE PIECE

INCORPORATING A LANDING

A high deck will require a very long flight of stairs. If you run them straight out, they will likely extend quite far into the yard or onto the lower level of the deck. To avoid this situation, you can incorporate one or more landings along the run. In the design shown here, the landing at the highest level allows the stairs to begin their descent parallel to the edge of the deck; the second landing partway down provides a pause in the flight. You can also use a landing to change the direction of the stairs. Build a landing in the same way as a small freestanding deck *(page 40)* and attach the stairs to it as you would to a deck.

A WHEELCHAIR RAMP

Framing for a sloping ramp.

The ramp at right consists of three section: a landing and two sloping modules with joists running along their length. The landing is set on two beams placed at the same height as the deck beams. A middle beam, partially buried, supports the bottom of the middle module and the top of the end module. An end beam, completely buried, is located at the end of the ramp. The joists of the end module are partially buried so their top edge meets a concrete slab at ground level at the end of the ramp. The number and length of the modules and the height of their beams depends on the height of the deck and the required slope *(page 74)*, but the modules should be equal in length and no longer than 8 feet.

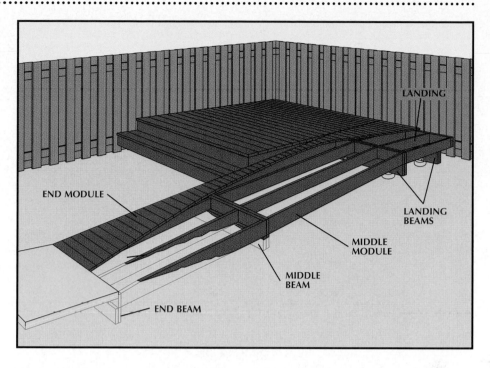

1. Setting the beams.

◆ Set up stakes and run two string lines parallel to the deck and at the same height as the deck surface: one 1 foot away from the deck and the second 3 feet away.
◆ Dig a trench at each buried-beam location, then cast cylindrical piers to support all four beams *(page 28)*, measuring down from the string line and moving the fiber-form tubes up and down to the appropriate height.
◆ Set post bases into the piers *(page 29)*, then fill the trenches with gravel up to the top of the piers.
◆ Make beams *(page 31)* 42 inches long, sit them in place *(above)*, and fasten them to the post bases *(page 33)*.

2. Building the landing.

◆ Construct a frame 42 inches square with four joists capped by two rim joints, fastening each joint with three $3\frac{1}{2}$-inch galvanized spiral-shank nails.
◆ Place the frame on the beams with an end joist against the deck and the outer face of one rim joist aligned with the center of the beam it will share with the middle module.
◆ Nail the end joist to the deck *(above)* and toenail each of the joists to the beams.

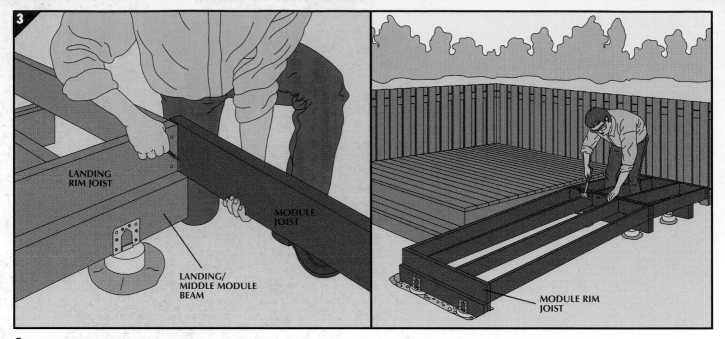

LANDING RIM JOIST

MODULE JOIST

LANDING/ MIDDLE MODULE BEAM

MODULE RIM JOIST

3. Installing the middle module.
◆ Holding a middle-module joist against the side of the landing platform with the other end resting on the middle beam, make a mark across the joist in line with the end of the landing's rim joist *(above, left)*.
◆ Cut the joist along the line, then trim the other end to length at the same angle.

◆ Use this joist as a template to mark and cut the remaining joists for both the middle and end modules.
◆ Cut the module rim joists 42 inches long, then assemble the middle module as you did the landing.
◆ Position the assembly on its beams, then fasten it to the landing platform with galvanized 3-inch nails spaced every 8 to 10 inches *(above, right)*.
◆ Toenail the module to the middle beam.

4. Installing the end module.
◆ Dig a shallow, progressively deeper trench for each end-module joist.
◆ Cut rim joists and assemble the end module as you did the middle one, then place it on the middle and end beams.
◆ Fasten the end module to the middle one and toenail it to the end beam.
◆ Fill in around the joists and beams with soil *(right)*.
◆ Cast a concrete slab 42 inches square at the end of the ramp *(page 75)*, its finished surface at a height that allows a smooth transition to the ramp.
◆ Install decking boards across the joists *(pages 62-63)*.

Decks higher than three steps generally require a railing, as do ramps and stairs with more than two risers. An important safety feature, the railing can also define the style of the deck (*below and page 93*).

Design Considerations: Per building codes, the handrail must be at least 36 inches above the deck surface, and gaps—such as between spindles or under the bottom rail— cannot exceed 4 inches. For a deck with 2-by-6 framing, buy 4-foot-long 4-by-4 posts. Otherwise, cut posts long enough to extend from the bottom of the rim or end joist to 42 inches above the deck surface. For a solid look, notch the posts and bolt them to the outside of the rim and end joists (*pages 84-86*). You can make the railings appear to be a more integral part of the deck by cutting through the decking boards and attaching the posts to the inside of the rim and end joists (*page 113, Step 1*) or by installing continuous posts (*page 35*).

Stairs and Gates: Design a stair railing to match the deck railing as closely as possible (*pages 91 and 93*). The handrail must be a type that is easy to grasp, set from 34 to 38 inches high—as measured from the back of the step's tread to the top of the handrail. Spindles can be spaced up to 4 inches apart; the gap below the bottom rail must not allow a 6-inch sphere to pass through. A gate at the top of the stairs is a sensible addition if the deck will be used by small children (*pages 94-95*).

TOOLS

Tape measure	Power miter saw
Combination square	Router
Carpenter's level (4')	Wood chisel
C-clamps	Mallet
Circular saw	Pry bar
	Electric drill
	Socket wrench

MATERIALS

Pressure-treated 1 x 2, 2 x 2s, 4 x 4s	Deck screws ($1\frac{1}{2}$", 2", $2\frac{1}{2}$")
Pressure-treated 2 x 6 or colonial-style handrail	Galvanized lag screws ($\frac{3}{8}$" x 3", 5") and washers
	Butt hinges (3" x 3")
	Swiveling caster
	Locking gate latch

SAFETY TIPS

Protect your eyes with goggles when using a power tool or hammering. Wear a dust mask when cutting pressure-treated wood; wash your hands thoroughly after handling it.

Two railing styles. The railings at right illustrate two different architectural styles. The colonial railing (*near right*) features commercial milled handrail stock with 2-by-2 spindles linking top and bottom rails; the assembly is set between 4-by-4 posts. Such a railing can span distances of up to 5 feet—10 feet if a support block is

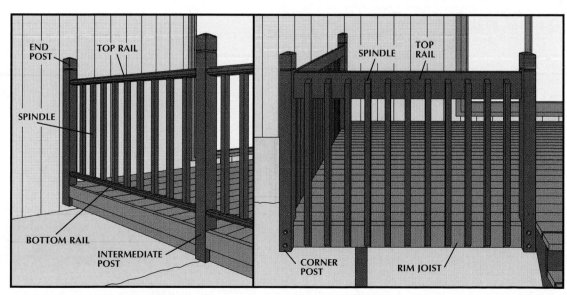

added in the middle of the span (*page 90*). If you plan to add a built-in bench (*pages 104-107*), substitute an intermediate post for the support block.

More difficult to climb than the colonial style, a traditional railing (*far right*) is a good choice for families with young children. This style has only a top rail, made either of ordinary 2-by-6 lumber or commercial milled 2-by-6 handrail stock. The spindles are attached to the handrail about $1\frac{1}{2}$ inches below the top, and to the outside face of the rim and end joists flush with the bottom. Intermediate posts are not required unless the deck will have a built-in bench along the railing; in this case, set posts every 5 feet for extra support.

SHAPING THE POSTS

Adding a chamfer and dado.
◆ With a combination square, draw two sets of lines all the way around each post, one $\frac{1}{2}$ inch from the top end and the second 3 inches away.
◆ Set the blade of a power miter saw to 15 degrees and cut all four faces of the post in line with the $\frac{1}{2}$-inch mark, forming a special bevel known as a chamfer.
◆ Clamp the post to a work surface, then equip a router with a $\frac{1}{2}$-inch straight bit. Adjust the depth to $\frac{1}{2}$ inch, align the bit with the 3-inch mark on the post, and position a wood block on the post flush against the router base. Screw the block to the post as a guide so its edges are perpendicular to the sides of the post, then cut a channel known as dado across the surface, feeding the router with its base against the guide.
◆ Remove the guide, rotate the post 90 degrees, and reposition the guide to rout dadoes across the post's remaining three sides *(right)*.

Instead of cutting chamfers and dadoes in the posts, you can top them with a decorative post cap such as the one in the photograph.

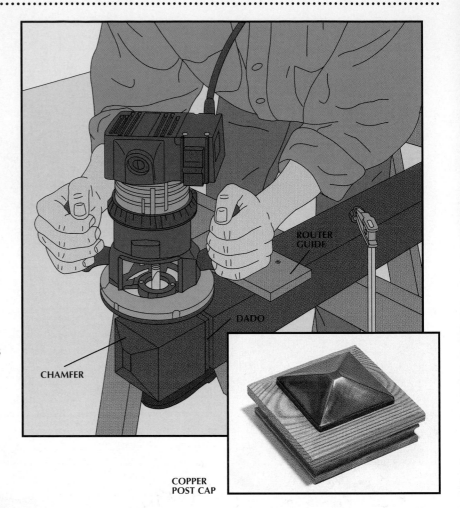

ROUTER GUIDE

DADO

CHAMFER

COPPER POST CAP

ATTACHING TO THE DECK

1. Notching the end posts.
◆ With a pencil and a combination square, outline a 2-inch-deep notch on one face of each end post at the bottom end, sizing its height to reach from the bottom of the end joist to the top of the decking.
◆ Cut along the lines with a circular saw *(right)* and clear out the waste piece with a pry bar.
◆ Clean up the cut with a mallet and a wood chisel.

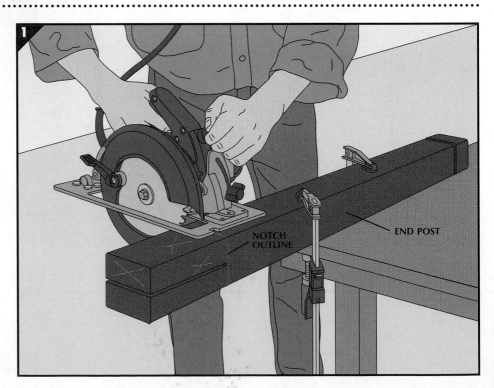

NOTCH OUTLINE

END POST

END POST

END JOIST

2. Installing the end post.

◆ Position the end post next to the house so the notch hugs the decking and the end joist.

◆ While a helper steadies the post, drill a pilot hole for a $\frac{3}{8}$- by 3-inch lag screw through the post and into the joist near the top edge, then fit a washer on the lag screw and drive it in.

◆ Have your helper plumb the post with a carpenter's level, then drive a second lag screw a few inches below the first *(left)*.

NOTCHING DECKING THAT OVERHANGS

Where the deck boards overhang the end joists, you will have to notch the decking to install the end posts. At each post location, mark a notch as wide as the post in line with the outer face of the end joist. Cut out the notch with a wood chisel and a mallet.

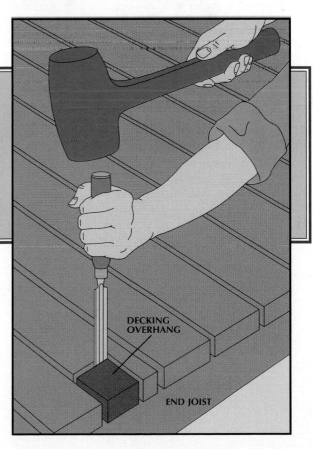

DECKING OVERHANG

END JOIST

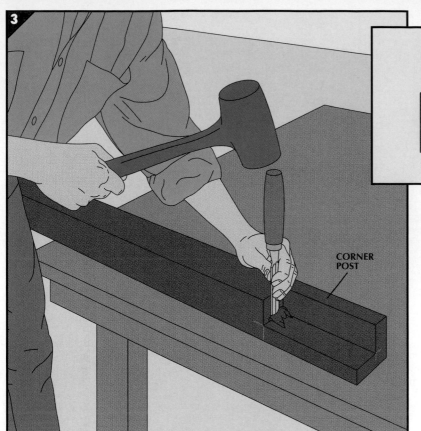

3. Preparing the corner posts.

◆ Outline a notch at the bottom end of each corner post, making it the same depth and height as those on the end posts *(page 84, Step 1)*, but at only one corner of the piece, rather than across its full width *(inset)*.

◆ Saw out the notch, then clean it up with a mallet and a wood chisel *(left)*.

4. Installing the corner post.

◆ Position the corner post, fitting its notch at the corner of the deck. Then, while a helper checks the post for plumb on two adjoining sides, fasten it to the rim and end joists with two $2\frac{1}{2}$-inch coated deck screws driven through each face. Tighten the screws alternately to keep the post plumb *(right)*.

◆ Fasten the post to the deck framing with lag screws as in Step 2, locating the screws on the two outer faces of the pieces; offset the screws so they won't hit each other.

5 TOP STAIR-
RAILING POST

STRINGER

RISER

5. Installing stair-railing posts.
◆ Notch a railing post for the top of the stairs as you would an end post *(page 84, Step 1)*.
◆ Position the post at the junction between one stair stringer and the deck, resting the top of the notch on the decking. Fasten the post in place *(page 85, Step 2)*.
◆ Place an unnotched post on the concrete slab at the bottom of the stairs, butting it against the stringer 2 inches back from the first riser. While a helper steadies and plumbs the post, drill pilot holes and fasten the post to the stringer with two $\frac{3}{8}$- by 5-inch galvanized lag screws and washers *(left)*.
◆ Install posts on the other side of the stairs in the same way.

If you have installed picture-frame steps, finish framing them *(page 80, Step 2)*.

CAPPING THE DECK EDGES

If the deck boards are flush with the outer sides of the end and rim joists, you can install a cap to conceal the decking. From the same type of wood used for the decking, cut a length of 5/4-by-4 stock to fit as a cap between each pair of railing posts. Fit the cap between two posts so its top edge is flush with the surface of the decking, then fasten it in place with $2\frac{1}{2}$-inch galvanized spiral-shank nails spaced every foot, driving them alternately into the joist and the decking.

CAP

JOIST

POST

A COLONIAL RAILING

1. Laying out the spindles.
◆ Cut two lengths of handrail and one filler strip to fit between each pair of posts.
◆ Wedge the lower rail and the strip between the posts so they are side by side on the deck and mark the middle of each piece.
◆ Cut a piece of spindle stock as a spacer, making it as long as the desired spindle spacing. Center it on-end on the mark and outline the center spindle on the rail and filler strip.
◆ Mark the edge of the next spindle by holding the spacer on one side and aligning an end with one of the center-spindle lines. Outline the spindle's other edge, then continue to lay out spindle locations until you have marked the last one at the post.
◆ Go back to the center-spindle outline and lay out the spindle locations between it and the opposite post *(right)*.

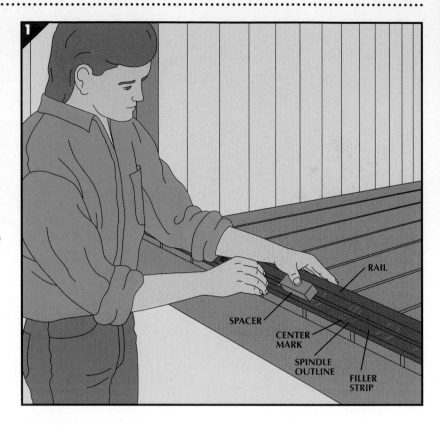

2. Cutting the spindles.
◆ Measure up from the decking and mark the position of the top of the upper rail *(left)*, then set a scrap of rail with a piece of filler strip *(inset)* at the mark and outline the bottom of the upper rail.
◆ Starting at the height of the bottom of the lower rail, lay out the position of the lower rail *(dashed lines)* using the same method, but omitting the filler strip.
◆ Measure the distance between the bottom of the top rail and the top of the bottom rail, then cut a spindle to length for each outline you made in Step 1. You can cut several pieces at once as described on page 79.

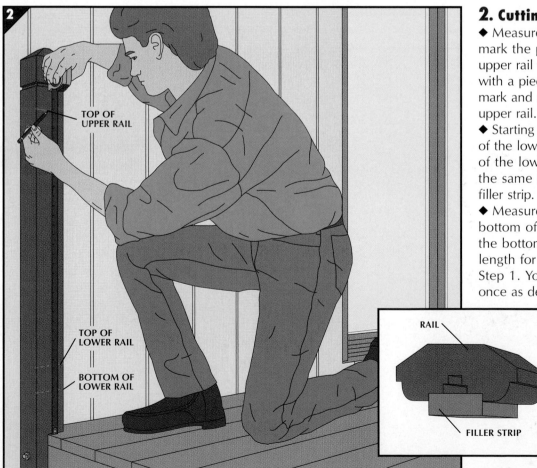

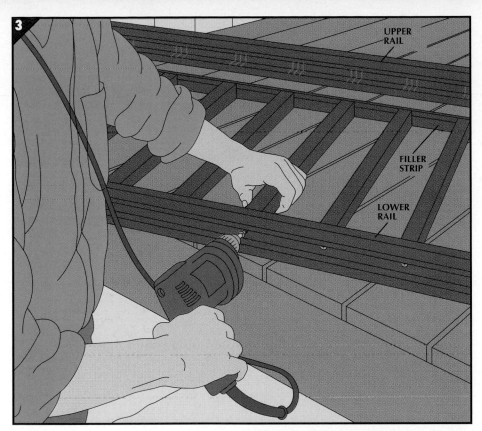

3. Assembling the railing.

◆ Drill a pilot hole for a 1½-inch coated deck screw through the filler strip at each marked spindle outline.

◆ Fasten the spindles to the filler strip.

◆ Attach the lower rail to the opposite end of the spindles in the same manner *(left)*.

4. Adding the upper rail.

◆ Turn the top rail upside down and set the assembly on top of it, fitting the filler strip into the groove in the rail and aligning the ends of the pieces.

◆ Drill a pilot hole for a 2-inch coated deck screw through the filler strip and into the handrail every 8 to 10 inches, then drive the screws *(right)*.

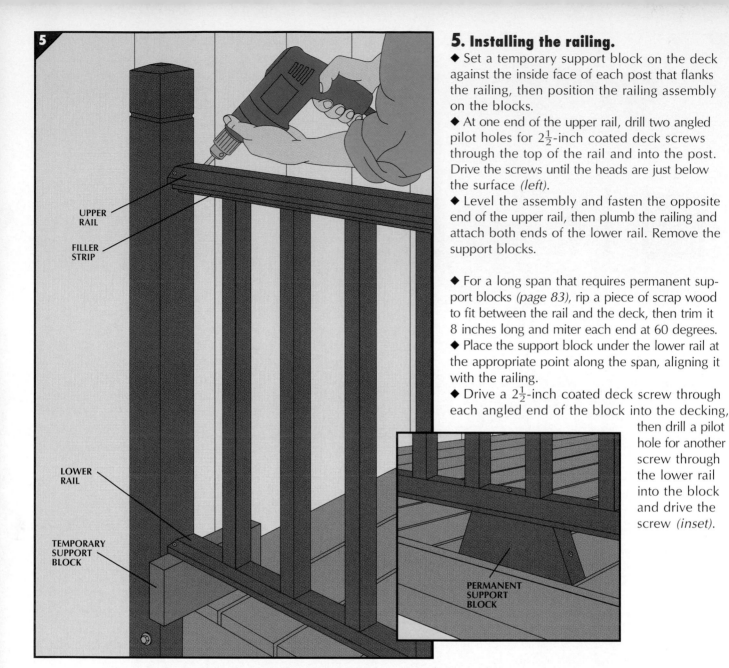

UPPER RAIL

FILLER STRIP

LOWER RAIL

TEMPORARY SUPPORT BLOCK

5. Installing the railing.

◆ Set a temporary support block on the deck against the inside face of each post that flanks the railing, then position the railing assembly on the blocks.

◆ At one end of the upper rail, drill two angled pilot holes for $2\frac{1}{2}$-inch coated deck screws through the top of the rail and into the post. Drive the screws until the heads are just below the surface (left).

◆ Level the assembly and fasten the opposite end of the upper rail, then plumb the railing and attach both ends of the lower rail. Remove the support blocks.

◆ For a long span that requires permanent support blocks (page 83), rip a piece of scrap wood to fit between the rail and the deck, then trim it 8 inches long and miter each end at 60 degrees.

◆ Place the support block under the lower rail at the appropriate point along the span, aligning it with the railing.

◆ Drive a $2\frac{1}{2}$-inch coated deck screw through each angled end of the block into the decking, then drill a pilot hole for another screw through the lower rail into the block and drive the screw (inset).

PERMANENT SUPPORT BLOCK

PREFABRICATED RAILINGS

An alternative to building your own railing is to buy prefabricated railing assemblies, such as the ones at right. The sections are fastened between railing posts in the same manner as the custom-made railings on these pages.

RAILING-HEIGHT MARK

HANDRAIL

POST

6. Fastening the stair railing.

◆ Lay a handrail on the steps and mark it where it meets the inside of each stair post *(inset)*. Adjust a power miter saw to the angle of the marks, then cut the rail to length.

◆ Cut another rail and a filler strip to the same length, beveling the ends at the same angle as the first rail.

◆ Cut spindles to the same height as those on the deck, beveling the ends at the angle of the rails.

◆ Assemble a railing section *(page 89, Steps 3 and 4)*, then place the section between the posts. Measuring from the back of an upper step, position the assembly so the handrail is at the correct height. Mark the upper post along the top of the rail.

◆ With a helper holding the railing assembly between the posts so the top of the handrail is even with the mark on the upper post, position the bottom end of the assembly so the handrail is at the same height relative to a lower step. Mark the lower post along the top of the rail *(left)*.

◆ With the railing section even with the marks, drill pilot holes for two $2\frac{1}{2}$-inch coated deck screws through the underside of the bottom end of the handrail and into the post. Drive the screws. Fasten the top end of the handrail by driving the screws through the top of the handrail.

◆ Plumb the assembly, then fasten both ends of the bottom rail in the same way.

A TRADITIONAL ALTERNATIVE

1. Laying out the spindles.

◆ Cut a 2-by-6 or a section of milled 2-by-6 railing to fit between a pair of posts.

◆ Lay out the location of the spindles *(page 88, Step 1)* along the top edge of the railing, then with a combination square, mark a line along the railing $1\frac{1}{2}$ inches from the top edge.

◆ Cut spindles to reach from the bottom of the rim or end joist to within $1\frac{1}{2}$ inches of the required height of the railing—at least 35 inches above the deck, beveling both ends at 45 degrees—you may be able to buy spindles of the right length with the ends already beveled.

◆ Drill two pilot holes for $2\frac{1}{2}$-inch coated deck screws through each spindle about 1 inch from the ends.

◆ Position the first spindle on the handrail within its outline and its top even with the line on the handrail, then screw it in place *(right)*.

◆ Fasten the last spindle to the opposite end of the handrail in the same way.

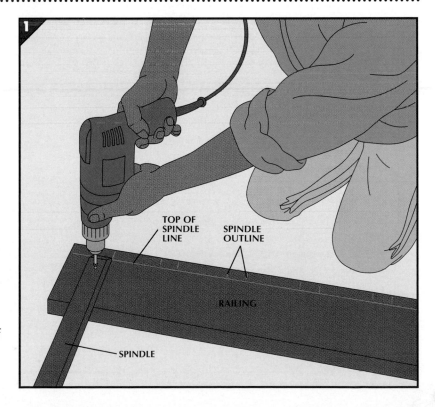

TOP OF SPINDLE LINE

SPINDLE OUTLINE

RAILING

SPINDLE

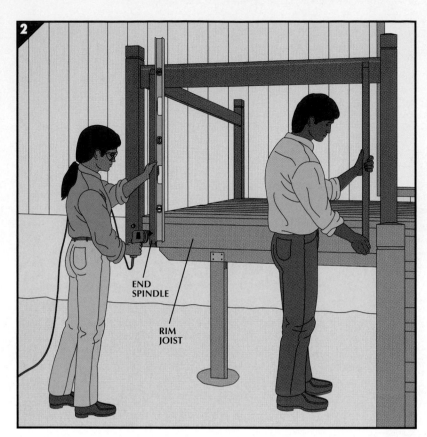

2. Mounting the railing.
◆ Place the railing assembly between the posts. With a helper holding one end spindle flush with the bottom of the rim or end joist, adjust the other end spindle so it is plumb and flush with the bottom of the joist.
◆ Fasten each spindle to the joist *(left)*.
◆ Plumb one of the end spindles, then drill two angled pilot holes for $2\frac{1}{2}$-inch coated deck screws through the face of the handrail and into the post at the same end. Then, drive the screws.
◆ Fasten the opposite end of the handrail in the same way.

END SPINDLE

RIM JOIST

3. Filling in the spindles.
◆ Secure the top of a spindle to the handrail at the second spindle location. Then, position the bottom of the spindle using the spacing block, and fasten the spindle to the joist.
◆ Continue adding spindles in the same way *(right)*. After installing four or five, fasten the top of the next one, then plumb it before attaching the bottom.
◆ Install the remaining spindles, plumbing every fourth or fifth one.

SPACER

4. Attaching the stair railing.

◆ Cut a 2-by-6 or a length of milled 2-by-6 railing as you would a colonial handrail *(page 91, Step 6)*, but align the ends of the rail with the outer sides of the posts.

◆ Position the handrail as described on page 91, Step 6, and, working with a helper, fasten the rail to the post with two $2\frac{1}{2}$-inch coated deck screws at each end *(left)*.

◆ Lay out the spindle locations on the rail *(page 88, Step 1)*, then cut the spindles to reach from the bottom of the stringer to $1\frac{1}{2}$ inches below the top edge of the handrail, cutting both ends to match the angle of the rails and beveling them at 45 degrees.

◆ Drill a pilot hole for a deck screw 1 inch from each end of the spindles.

◆ Fasten the spindles to the stringer and handrail *(opposite, Step 3)*.

DISTINCTIVE RAILINGS

The primary restrictions in designing a deck railing are that the plan meet all code requirements and the railing be supported by an adequate number of posts to prevent it from flexing and sagging. Following these guidelines, you can choose among any number of styles to complement your deck. Two distinctive railings are featured in the photographs below. The one at left has vertical slats of alternating 2-by-2s and 1-by-4s, and the pattern along the top augments the Japanese motif. The railing at right represents the style known as Craftsman. Its heaviness is softened by the sweeping curve of the handrail. This particular structure has continuous posts *(page 35)*.

1. Assembling the gate.

◆ Build the gate in the same way as a railing section *(pages 88-89)*, but with two spindles side by side at each end. Size the gate to fit between the posts at the top of the stairs with a $\frac{1}{4}$-inch gap on each side.

◆ Make two vertical braces of 1-by-4 stock: Cut them to fit between the rails and rip them to the same width as the doubled spindles.

◆ Lay the gate down inside-face up and attach the 1-by-4s to the end spindles with $1\frac{1}{2}$-inch coated deck screws, aligning the edges of the pieces *(right)*.

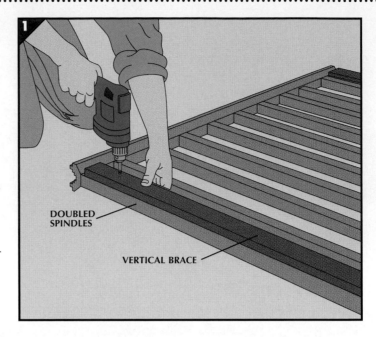

DOUBLED SPINDLES

VERTICAL BRACE

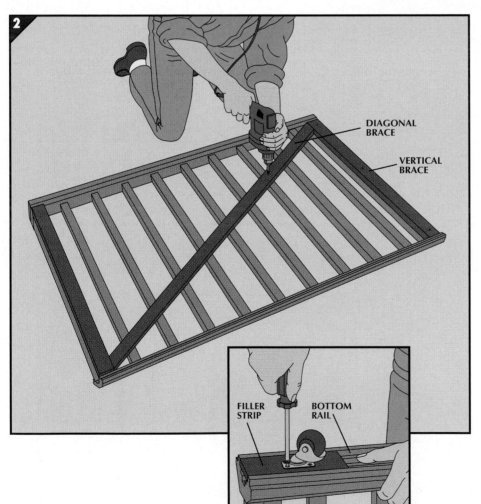

DIAGONAL BRACE

VERTICAL BRACE

FILLER STRIP

BOTTOM RAIL

2. Bracing the gate.

◆ Fasten a 1-by-2 brace diagonally between the vertical ones so it runs from the top of the gate's latch side to the bottom of the hinge side. Drive a $1\frac{1}{2}$-inch coated deck screw through the brace into every other spindle and into each vertical brace *(left)*.

◆ Position one leaf of a 3- by 3-inch butt hinge on the hinge-side of the gate, locating it 4 inches from the top and so the gate will swing onto the deck. Mark the screw holes, remove the hinge, drill a pilot hole for a screw at each mark, then fasten the hinge to the gate.

◆ Attach a second hinge 4 inches from the bottom of the gate.

◆ Cut a filler strip 8 inches long and position it on the bottom rail at the latch side of the gate.

◆ Drill a pilot hole for a deck screw through the filler strip at each spindle location, then drive the screws.

◆ Fasten a swiveling caster to the filler strip near the latch edge *(inset)*.

3. Hanging the gate.
◆ Position the gate between the stair posts, have a helper hold it level, then mark the free screw holes of the top hinge on the post *(left)*.
◆ Fasten the hinge leaf to the post, then attach the bottom hinge.

4. Adding the latch.
◆ Position the strike 3 inches from the top on the latch-side vertical brace of the gate, mark its screw holes, drill pilot holes, and fasten the strike in place.
◆ Engage the strike with the latch, then close the gate.
◆ Mark the latch's screw holes and screw it to the post *(right)*.

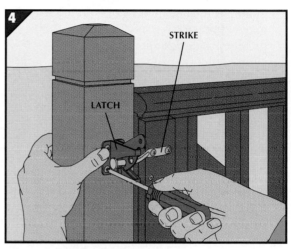

A TRADITIONAL GATE

Assembling the gate.
◆ Cut a 2-by-6 handrail and a length of 2-by-4 to fit between the stair posts, with a $\frac{1}{4}$-inch gap on each side.
◆ Lay out spindle locations *(page 88, Step 1)* on both pieces, adding marks for double spindles at each end.
◆ Cut spindles to reach from the bottom of the 2-by-4 to $1\frac{1}{2}$ inches below the top of the handrail when the gate is assembled, then fasten the spindles to the two pieces as described on page 92, Step 3.
◆ Cut two 2-by-4s to the planned height of the gate, beveling the ends, and cut them 3 inches wide as vertical braces.
◆ With $2\frac{1}{2}$-inch coated deck screws, fasten the braces to the inside face of the gate assembly flush with the outer edges.
◆ Add a diagonal 2-by-2 brace *(opposite, Step 2)*, then add a caster, hang the gate, and install a latch as for a colonial gate.

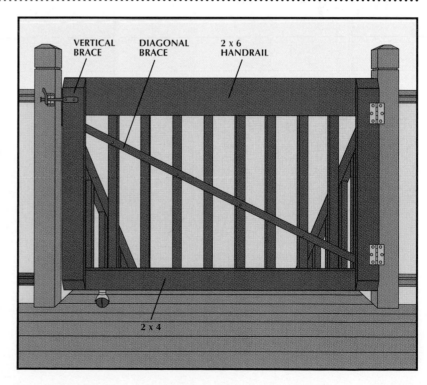

VERTICAL BRACE   DIAGONAL BRACE   2 x 6 HANDRAIL

2 x 4

Protecting the Deck with a Finish

Nature can take a toll on a deck. Water can cause the wood to warp and crack; the ultraviolet (UV) rays of the sun can change its color; mildew can stain it; and fungus and insects may attack it. Although the deck understructure generally does not need to be finished, the decking, railings, and other details may need a protective coating formulated to defend the wood against one or more of these enemies. The ideal finish for a deck depends on local climate, the type of wood, and the desired appearance. Some areas have strict controls on the level of volatile organic compounds (VOCs) in finishes. In the absence of such regulations, select a finish marked "VOC compliant."

Pressure-Treated Wood: Designed to resist fungus and insects, this type of wood lasts longer if it is coated with a water-repellent finish; for best results, choose one that also contains a mildewcide. A clear water repellent with UV protection will preserve the color of the wood; without UV protection, it will weather to gray. To change the color or mask the green tint of some pressure-treated woods, use a tinted water repellent or a semi-transparent stain. Do not paint a deck—paint wears quickly and refinishing is difficult.

Redwood and Cedar: Boards milled from the tree heartwood—the generally darker wood around the middle of the trunk—is naturally resistant to fungus and insects; it requires only a water repellent containing a mildewcide. For lumber that contains some sapwood—the lighter-colored wood surrounding the heartwood—use a finish that also includes preservatives that guard against fungus and insects. A finish with UV protection will maintain the natural color of the boards, whereas one without it will let them weather to gray. Since redwood and cedar are often chosen for their natural beauty, they are not usually stained.

Finishing and Refinishing: In general, wait three or four weeks—but no more than a month, depending on the manufacturer's requirements—after the deck is built before applying a finish. Choose a cool, windless day for the job, and make sure the wood is completely dry.

Regular maintenance *(below)* will increase the life of a deck. To determine if it is time for refinishing, check if water beads on the surface or soaks in. If the latter, refinish the deck.

⚠ CAUTION *To avoid spontaneous combustion of rags or rollers soaked with finish, dry them outside, then store them in a sealed glass or metal container.*

 TOOLS

Broom
Paintbrush
Paint roller and extension pole
Roller tray

 **MATERIALS**

Deck finish

 SAFETY TIPS

Put on gloves when applying a deck finish; add goggles if using a sprayer.

A Maintenance Checklist

✔ Sweep the deck regularly so debris doesn't block drainage between deck boards. With a putty knife, clear out any debris that collects between boards.

✔ Hose the deck down periodically so dirt isn't ground into the finish.

✔ Move furniture and other accessories occasionally to allow the deck surface to dry thoroughly.

✔ Check for popped nails and reset them.

✔ Refinish the deck as required—generally about every two years.

✔ To check for wood rot, drive an awl or a sharp knife into framing members where they meet each other or the ground. If the tool penetrates easily, replace the affected piece.

✔ Inspect the deck for signs of insect damage such as tiny holes or pitted surfaces. If necessary, consult a pest-control expert.

Applying the finish.

◆ Sweep the deck surface clean.

◆ With the type of paintbrush recommended by the finish manufacturer, first apply the product to the deck railing and any other details. Working in small sections, apply a second coat of finish before the first dries. Apply up to three additional coats to end grain. After the finish has dried for about an hour, wipe up or brush in wet spots.

◆ Finish the decking in the same manner, but with a paint roller and an extension pole *(left)*. To speed the application of the finish, you can buy a pressure sprayer *(below)*.

PRESSURE SPRAYING FOR A QUICK FINISH

A pressure sprayer can greatly speed up the job of applying a deck finish, particularly on detailed parts such as railings. Be sure to buy a sprayer that is intended for finishes, not pesticides or other garden chemicals. With its large two-gallon tank, the model shown at right has sufficient capacity to cover 300 to 500 square feet without refilling. The nozzle is designed to give an even, flat spray pattern that resembles a brush stroke.

Benches, Planters, Screens, and Skirts

Although a bare deck may be perfectly serviceable, a few additional details will make it feel really homey. Built-in benches provide convenient seating, planters allow you to brighten the deck with flowers and shrubs, and overheads and screens provide shade and privacy. Skirting the outside of a high deck turns unused space into convenient storage.

Attaching a back slat to a deck bench →

Benches provide permanent seating on a deck, and can be supplemented by outdoor furniture. Built-in units can define areas for eating or conversation, guide traffic flow, or break up long expanses of railing.

Styles: On a low deck, you can build a simple backless bench around the perimeter *(below)*. For a higher level, position such a bench against the railing or build a sloping back that is attached to the railing posts *(pages 104-107)*.

You can also close in the structure to create a storage area *(pages 102-103)*. With either style, make the seat slats of lumber that complements other deck features, such as the decking and stair treads.

Designing for Comfort: Build benches from 15 to 18 inches high, and make seats 12 to 15 inches deep. Slope bench backs at about 15 degrees, with the back slat 12 inches above the seat.

TOOLS

Combination square
Carpenter's square

Circular saw
Electric drill
Screwdriver
Hand plane

MATERIALS

Pressure-treated
 2 x 2s, 2 x 4s,
 2 x 6s

Plywood ($\frac{1}{8}$")
Pressure-treated
 5/4 x 4 stock
Deck screws ($2\frac{1}{2}$")
Butt hinges (3" x 3")

SAFETY TIPS

Put on goggles when using a power tool. Add a dust mask to cut pressure-treated wood, and wash your hands thoroughly after handling the wood.

A BACKLESS BENCH

Anatomy of the bench.

The bench at right has a frame made of 2-by-6s beveled at the corners. The frame is sized to accommodate seven 2-by-2 seat slats with $\frac{1}{8}$-inch gaps between them, but you can use any combination of 2-by-2s, 2-by-4s, or 2-by-6s that adds up to a comfortable seat depth. The slats are held up by 2-by-4 seat supports set $1\frac{1}{2}$ inches below the top of the frame every 16 inches. This bench, which can be built up to 6 feet long, has end legs made of two 2-by-4s with a 2-by-2 cleat between them that secures the structure to the decking. To make a longer bench, add more leg assemblies to provide adequate support.

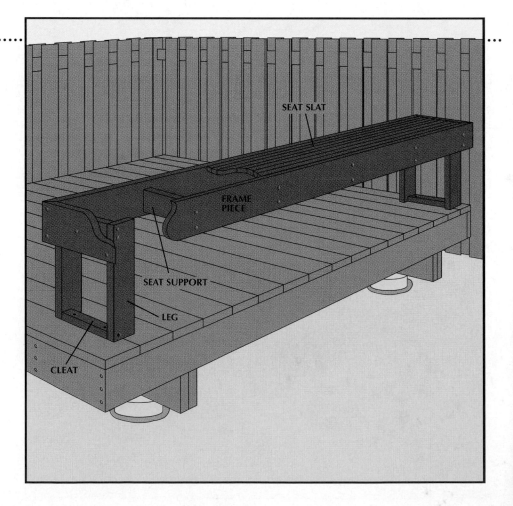

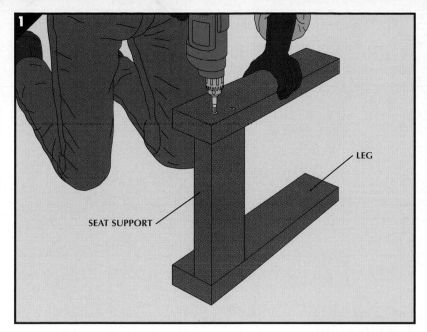

1. Building the leg assembles.

◆ For each end of the bench, cut two 2-by-4 legs to the desired height of the bench less $1\frac{1}{2}$ inches.

◆ Cut a seat support to the planned inside width of the frame less 3 inches— 9 inches for a seat 12 inches wide.

◆ Attach the legs to the seat support so the top edge of the support is flush with the tops of the legs and one side aligns with the legs' outer edges *(left)*; drive two $2\frac{1}{2}$-inch coated deck screws through each leg into the end of the seat support.

2. Attaching the frame.

◆ Cut four 2-by-6s, beveling the ends at 45 degrees, to form a frame with the desired inside width—here, 9 inches—and length.

◆ Fasten each joint with two deck screws.

◆ Fit a leg assembly into each end of the frame and, working with a helper, set the bench upright.

◆ While the helper holds the end in place, set a 2-by-2 scrap on one leg assembly and position the frame so the top edge of the 2-by-2 is flush with the top of the frame.

◆ Fasten the frame to each leg with two deck screws *(right)*.

◆ Attach the other leg assembly in the same way.

◆ Round the beveled corners of the frame slightly with a hand plane.

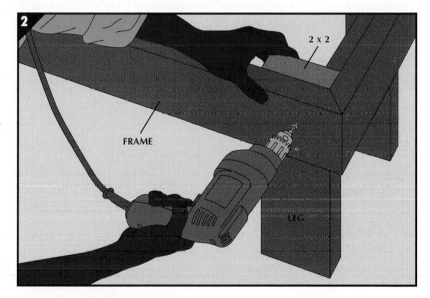

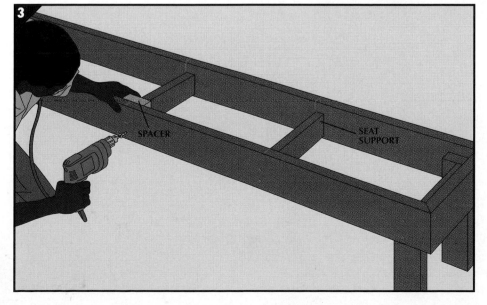

3. Adding seat supports.

◆ On each side of the frame, make a mark every 16 inches. With a combination square, transfer the marks to the inner face of the frame.

◆ For each marked location, cut a 2-by-4 seat support to fit across the inside of the frame.

◆ Place a seat support in the frame, aligning it with its mark.

◆ Holding a short 2-by-2 spacer with its bottom edge on the support and its top edge flush with the top of the frame, drive two deck screws through the frame into each end of the support.

◆ Install the remaining seat supports in the same way *(left)*.

4. Fastening the seat slats.

◆ Cut the seat slats to length, then set them in place astride their supports.
◆ Cut a $\frac{1}{8}$-inch plywood spacer, slip it between the frame and the first slat over an end seat support, and drill a pilot hole for a deck screw through the slat into the support; drill two holes if you are laying 2-by-4 or 2-by-6 slats. Make an additional hole where the slat and each remaining one crosses a support (right), moving the spacer along as you go.
◆ Drive the screws.

SPACER

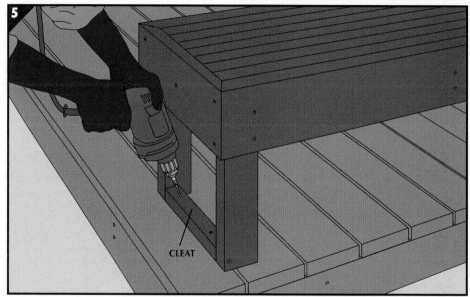

CLEAT

5. Anchoring the bench.

◆ Position the bench on the deck, then cut a 2-by-2 cleat to fit between each set of legs.
◆ Position a cleat between one set of bench legs, flush with their outside edge, and attach each leg to the end of it with one deck screw.
◆ Fasten the cleat to the decking with three deck screws.
◆ Install the other cleat in the same way (left).

CREATING A STORAGE AREA

1. Marking the lid.

◆ Construct a backless bench following Steps 1 to 3 on page 101, making it $16\frac{3}{4}$ inches high and sizing it to hold 2-by-4 or 2-by-6 seat slats.
◆ Cut the slats to length and set them in place.
◆ With a carpenter's square, mark a line across the boards to indicate the sides of a hinged lid, locating each line over a seat support (right). Make the lid no longer than 32 inches.
◆ Label the slats so you can put them back in the same locations after cutting them.

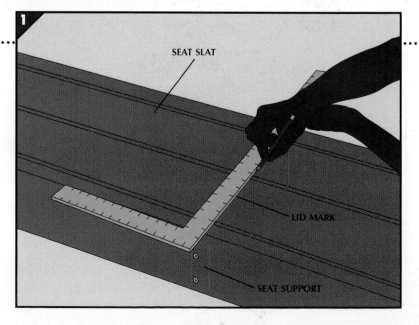

SEAT SLAT

LID MARK

SEAT SUPPORT

2. Making and hinging the lid.
◆ Remove the slats and cut them along the lines.
◆ Place the pieces that will form the lid face down, spacing them $\frac{1}{8}$ inch apart, and draw a line across their middle.
◆ Cut two 2-by-6 and two 2-by-2 cleats as long as the combined width of the slats and set them across the slats, positioning the 2-by-6s $1\frac{1}{2}$ inches from each end and the 2-by-2s 1 inch on each side of the center line.
◆ Fasten the cleats as shown in the inset.
◆ Install the fixed slats at each end of the bench *(opposite, Step 4)*.
◆ Put the lid in place and attach it with three 3- by 3-inch galvanized butt hinges *(page 73)*, placing a hinge 6 inches from each end *(right)* and a third hinge in between.

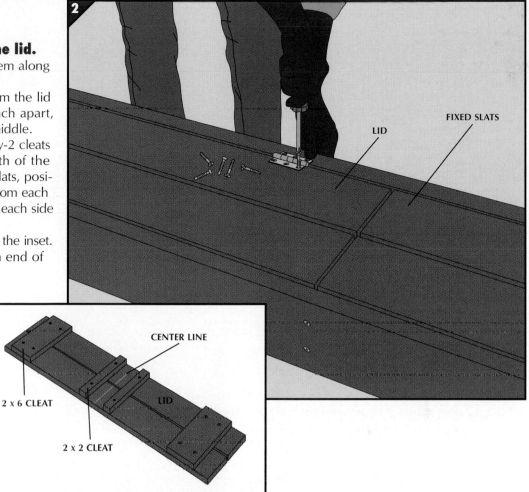

3. Closing in the sides.
◆ Anchor the bench to the deck *(opposite, Step 5)*.
◆ Cut two 2-by-6s to the same length as the side pieces of the frame *(page 101, Step 2)*, beveling the ends.
◆ Set one piece on the deck against the legs and fasten it to each leg with two deck screws.
◆ Attach the second piece in the same way.
◆ Cut two end pieces to fit between the sides, beveling the ends. Fasten each one with two deck screws driven into each side piece.
◆ Add another tier of 2-by-6s, leaving the same gap above and below the boards *(left)*.
◆ Round the beveled corners of the frame slightly with a hand plane.

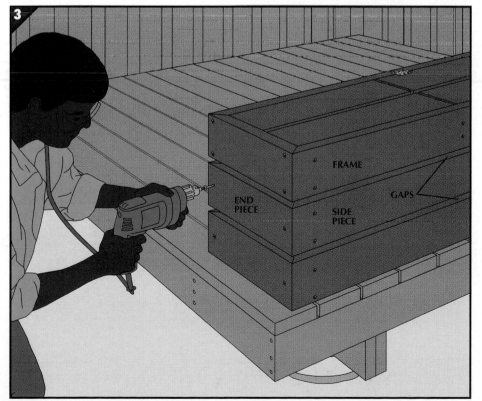

A BENCH WITH A BACK

Anatomy of the bench.

This bench at right is attached to the railing posts, which can be no more than 5 feet apart. At each post, the bench is supported by a leg assembly consisting of a back support, a seat support, and a leg. The supports at the two ends are the mirror image of each other—in each case, the seat support is fastened to the inside faces of the back support and leg. The top and bottom of the back supports are cut at 15-degree angles, which tilts the back slightly. The design shown consists of two 2-by-6 seat slats, but any combination of 2-by-4s and 2-by-6s that add up to a comfortable seat depth can be used; simply adjust the length of the seat support to accommodate the combined width of the slats with a $\frac{1}{8}$-inch gap between each. The seat is capped with 5/4-by-4 stock for a finished look. The back slat is a single 2-by-6, but a 2-by-8 or two 2-by-4s could be used for a broader back.

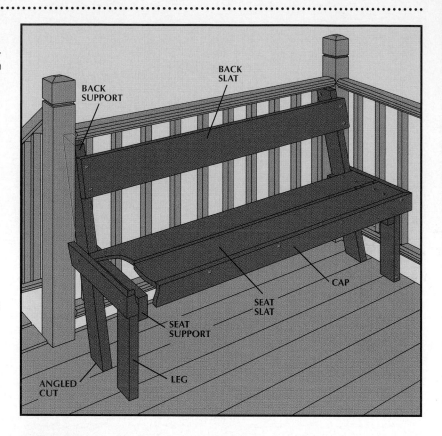

1. Cutting the back support.
◆ Cut a 2-by-4 back support about 4 feet long, mitering one end at 15 degrees.
◆ Set the angled end of the 2-by-4 on the deck and slip the other end through the deck railing and hold it against the outside of the handrail.
◆ Draw a line across the front edge of the 2-by-4 along the underside of the handrail (above), then miter the board along the line at 15 degrees.

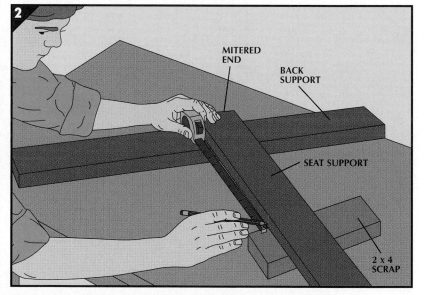

2. Cutting the seat support and leg.
◆ Cut a 2-by-4 seat support about 2 feet long, mitering one end at 15 degrees.
◆ Set the seat support on the back support, aligning the mitered end with the rear edge of the back support and resting the other end on a 2-by-4 scrap.
◆ Measuring from the front edge of the back support, mark the top edge of the seat support at the desired depth of the seat (above)—11$\frac{1}{8}$ inches in this example.
◆ Saw the seat support square at the mark.
◆ Cut a 2-by-4 leg 1$\frac{1}{2}$ inches shorter than the desired height of the seat.

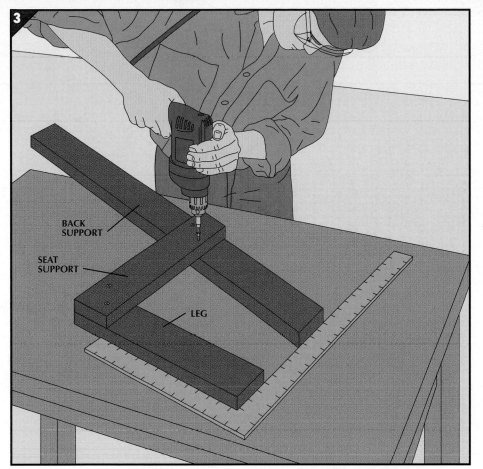

3. Putting the assembly together.

◆ Set the back support and leg flat on a work surface and place the seat support on top so the bottoms of the leg and back support are aligned, the square end of the seat support is flush with the front edge of the leg, and the mitered end is flush with the rear edge of the back support.

◆ Fasten the seat support to the back support and the leg with two deck screws at each joint *(left)*.

◆ Construct a second leg assembly for the other end of the bench, assembling the pieces as the mirror image of the first.

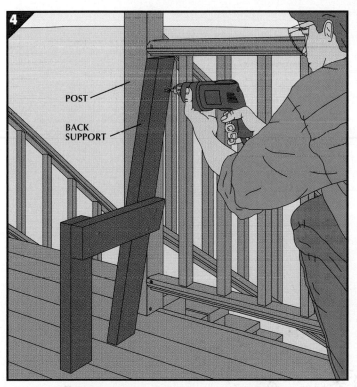

4. Mounting the leg assemblies.

◆ Position each leg assembly against the inside of the railing post and fasten it to the post with two deck screws through the back support *(above, left)*.

◆ Square the leg assembly on the decking with a carpenter's square, then mark the leg's position.

◆ Keeping the leg on the mark, drive a deck screw at an angle through the leg's front edge into the decking *(above, right)*.

◆ Fasten the other leg in the same manner.

BACK SUPPORT

SEAT SLAT

SEAT
SUPPORT

LEG

5. Fastening the seat slats.
◆ Cut two seat slats to length.
◆ Position one slat at the back of the bench and attach it to each seat support with two deck screws.
◆ Fasten the second slat in the same way, lining up its outer edge with the front ends of the seat supports *(left)*.

If the seat design calls for more than two slats, space the additional ones evenly between the front and back slats.

6. Adding the back slat.
◆ Cut a 2-by-6 to the same length as the seat slats.
◆ Draw a line on each back support 12 inches above the seat.
◆ Align the bottom of the back slat with the marks, then fasten the slat to each back support with two deck screws *(right)*.

BACK SLAT

BACK
SUPPORT

7. Capping the seat.

◆ Miter one end of a 5/4-by-4 board at 15 degrees as an end cap, then position it against the outer faces of a leg and back support so the mitered end lines up with the rear edge of the back support. Mark the other end of the cap where it meets the outer edge of the seat slats.

◆ Make a 45-degree bevel cut at this mark that will accommodate a beveled cap at the front of the seat *(inset)*.

◆ Reposition the end cap flush with the top of the seat slats and fasten it to the back support and the leg with two deck screws.

◆ Mount an end cap at the other end of the bench.

◆ Cut a front-cap piece to fit between the end caps, beveling both ends at 45 degrees, and fasten it to the front seat slat with a deck screw driven every 8 inches *(right)*.

◆ Lock the corners with two screws driven through the front cap into each end cap.

◆ Round the beveled corners of the frame slightly with a hand plane.

BENCH AND RAILING IN ONE

Instead of attaching a bench to an existing railing as described above, you can build a bench with a sloping back that doubles as a railing, using commercial deck brackets that hold the supports out from the deck at a slight angle. Make sure your design meets code requirements for railings *(page 83)*. As shown at right, bolt the brackets to the end or rim joist and slip the back supports into the brackets. Fasten the seat slats to the deck brackets and back slats to the back support.

Planters

Besides providing plants and flowers with a place to grow, deck planters can serve several other functions. They can be positioned to accentuate a change in levels *(box, below)*, to soften the transition between the deck and the yard, or to create a border for a low-level deck. They can also divide areas of activity on a single level. Pairs of planters can frame a doorway or the top of a stairway, or flank the ends of a bench. They are a practical alternative to flower pots, and can be built in a variety of shapes and sizes to fulfill different purposes.

Design Considerations: To build a unit to hold small plantings, you can add a sturdy false bottom to reduce the amount of soil it requires. You may want to fasten a planter to the deck in a permanent location, or place it on casters so it can be moved. Build the units from rot-resistant wood, but avoid stock that has been treated with creosote, which is harmful to plants.

 TOOLS

Carpenter's square
Circular saw
Electric drill

 MATERIALS

Pressure-treated
   2 x 2s, 2 x 4s, 1 x 6s
Pressure-treated
   5/4 x 4 stock
Deck screws (2", $2\frac{1}{2}$")

 SAFETY TIPS

Protect your eyes with goggles when using power tools. Put on a dust mask when cutting pressure-treated wood, and wash your hands thoroughly after handling the wood.

ACCENTUATING A LEVEL CHANGE

In this design, a set of broad steps makes the transition between two levels. A double-decker planter rests on the lower level and rises high enough to frame the end of the entire flight of steps. It also blends naturally into the adjacent yard plantings.

BUILDING A PLANTER

Anatomy of a planter.

The planter at right has four side panels of 1-by-6s held together with 2-by-2 cleats at the bottom and 2-by-4 cleats at the top. The side panels can also be made of 1-by-4s or 1-by-8s, depending on the overall dimensions of the planter. Two more cleats on opposite sides support a false bottom made of boards that are set on the cleats with gaps between them for drainage. On a rectangular planter, locate the cleats on the long sides. In this example, the false bottom is halfway up the sides, but it can be set at any height. A cap and strips of outer banding are added around the top. The planter can be fastened to the deck through the bottom cleats.

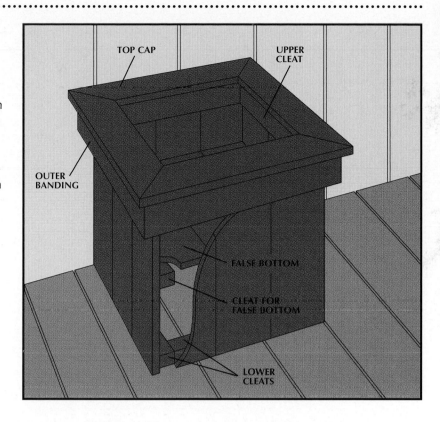

TOP CAP

UPPER CLEAT

OUTER BANDING

FALSE BOTTOM

CLEAT FOR FALSE BOTTOM

LOWER CLEATS

1. Making the side panels.

◆ Cut the boards to length for all four side panels, then lay out the boards for one panel, aligning the ends.

◆ Saw two 2-by-2 cleats 5 inches shorter than the panel width, center a cleat on the panel between the edges and flush with one end, and fasten the cleat to each board with two 2-inch coated deck screws (inset, left).

◆ Assemble a second panel in the same way.

◆ Put the remaining two side panels together with cleats only 1 inch shorter than the panel width and flush with one edge rather than centered between the edges (inset, right).

◆ With a carpenter's square, draw a line across the inner side of each of these last two panels at the appropriate height for the false bottom (left).

◆ Cut two cleats 2 inches shorter than the panel width, center each one along the marked line, then fasten it in place.

BOTTOM CLEAT

PANEL

CLEAT FOR FALSE BOTTOM

CLEATS

PANEL WITH CENTERED CLEAT   PANEL WITH OFFSET CLEAT

2. Assembling the panels.

◆ Assemble the panel as shown in the inset. Hold a panel with an offset cleat against one with a centered cleat so the cleat and panel butt against the inner face of the side and the sides form a 90-degree angle, then fasten them together with three deck screws.

◆ Add the remaining panel with an offset cleat so its inner face butts against the edge of the centered-cleat side *(right)*, then fasten the last centered-cleat panel.

◆ Position the planter on the deck and, if desired, anchor it to the decking with two $2\frac{1}{2}$-inch coated deck screws driven through each bottom cleat.

◆ Cut the required number of 1-by boards for the false bottom to length, sawing them to width to maintain $\frac{1}{8}$-inch gaps between them, then place them on their cleats.

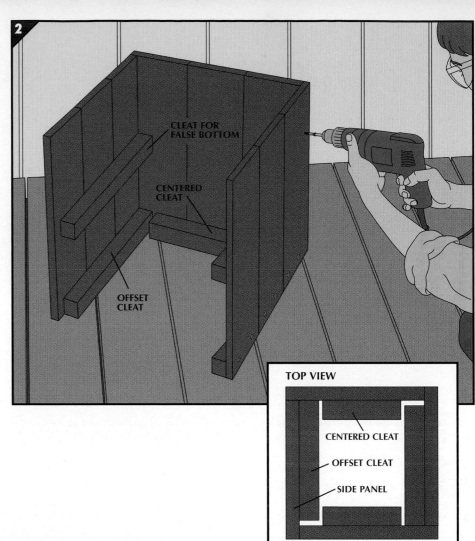

CLEAT FOR FALSE BOTTOM

CENTERED CLEAT

OFFSET CLEAT

TOP VIEW

CENTERED CLEAT

OFFSET CLEAT

SIDE PANEL

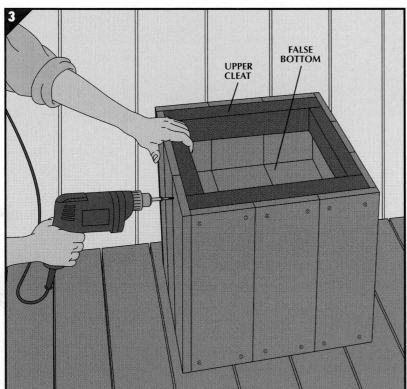

UPPER CLEAT

FALSE BOTTOM

3. Fastening the upper cleats.

◆ Cut two 2-by-4 cleats to the inside width of the planter, position one of them across a side panel with its upper edge flush with the top, and fasten it in place with two 2-inch coated deck screws driven through each board.

◆ Attach the second cleat to the opposite panel in the same way.

◆ Cut two more cleats to fit between the first pair and fasten them in place *(left)*.

Containing Soil

The gaps in the false bottom of a planter are designed to let water escape easily, since good drainage is necessary for plants to thrive; however, soil may leak out as well. To keep soil contained in a planter, place plastic sheeting on the false bottom and sides before you add the top cap *(Step 4)*. Staple the sheeting to the upper cleats *(right)*, then trim off the excess with scissors. Punch a few small holes in the plastic to allow adequate drainage.

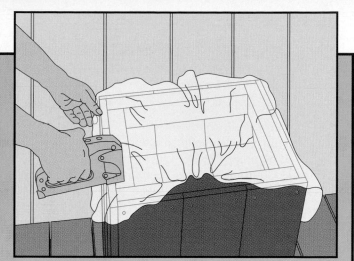

4. Anchoring the top cap.

◆ Cut four pieces of 5/4-by-4 stock to cap the top of the planter, mitering the corners so the joints will align with the corners of the planter.
◆ Fasten one piece to an upper cleat with $2\frac{1}{2}$-inch coated deck screws spaced about every 6 inches so the mitered ends are in line with the corners and the inner edge is flush with the inner face of the cleat *(right)*.
◆ Add the remaining three pieces, pulling each corner joint tight.
◆ Pin each corner with a screw driven through one side of the joint.

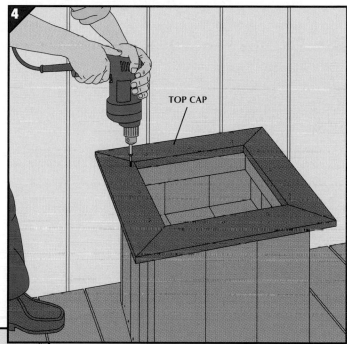

TOP CAP

5. Adding the outer banding.

◆ Cut four pieces of 5/4-by-4 stock to fit as banding around the planter under the top cap, beveling the ends.
◆ Fasten the banding pieces in place, driving deck screws spaced about every 6 inches through the sides and into the upper cleats *(left)*.
◆ Pin the corners with two screws driven through one side of each joint.

When you want a shady retreat from the sun, you can build an overhead that blends with the style of the deck. Combined with screens *(page 116-119)*, or vines trailing over it, such a structure can take on the feel of a cozy outdoor room that offers privacy as well as shade. As with the deck, make sure the design of the overhead meets all local code requirements.

Posts: If you are building a new deck, fasten the posts to the joists before you install the adjacent decking boards; on an existing deck, you'll need to remove these boards temporarily to access the framing. An alternative to attaching the posts to joists is to build the deck itself with continuous posts *(page 35)* that serve the additional purpose of supporting the overhead.

Slats: The amount of shade provided by the overhead will depend on the size and spacing of the slats. Buy a few of various sizes and experiment with positioning them until you have determined the ideal size and spacing for your project. If you decide to use slats that are 2-by-2, do not buy the lot until you are ready to install them, since they tend to warp quickly when not fastened down.

 TOOLS

Combination square

Carpenter's level (4')

Circular saw

Saber saw

Electric drill

Hammer

Wrenches

 MATERIALS

Pressure-treated 1 x 6s, 2 x 2s, 2 x 6s, 4 x 4s

Galvanized spiral-shank nails ($3\frac{1}{2}$")

Deck screws ($2\frac{1}{2}$")

Galvanized lag screws ($\frac{3}{8}$" x 5") and washers

Galvanized carriage bolts ($\frac{1}{2}$" x 7") and washers

 SAFETY TIPS

Wear goggles when using power tools or hammering. Put on a dust mask to cut pressure-treated wood, and wash your hands thoroughly after handling the wood.

Anatomy of an overhead.

Supported by 4-by-4 corner posts bolted to the end and rim joists of the deck, the overhead at right is designed much like a deck. In this example, 2-by-2 slats are laid across 2-by-6 split rafters resting on 2-by-6 split beams. The beams and end rafters are bolted to the posts, and the middle rafter is anchored to the beams with short posts. The deck boards are notched to accommodate the posts, whose bases have decorative cladding.

Like a deck, an overhead is engineered from the top down. The rafters can be spaced no more than 4 feet apart, and the posts no more than 10. The beams must be located at least 6 feet, 8 inches, above the deck surface.

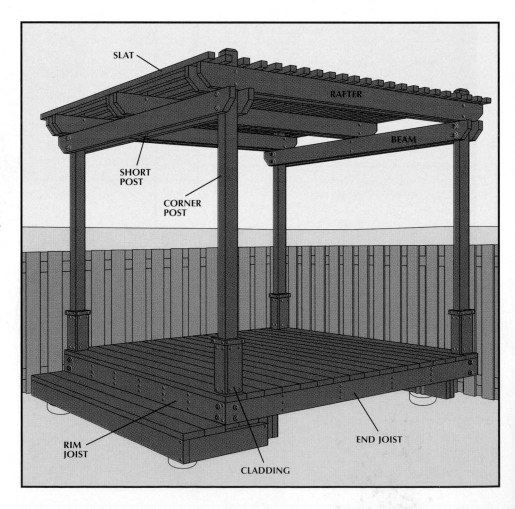

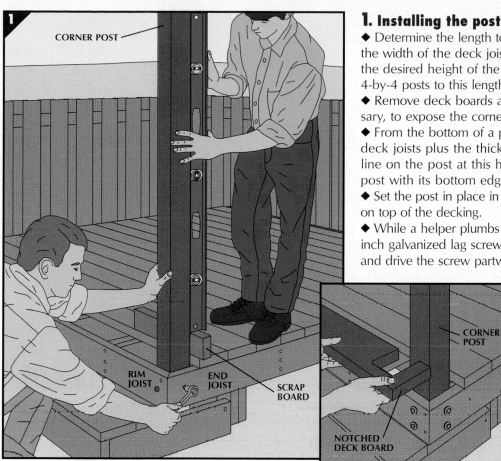

CORNER POST

RIM JOIST • END JOIST • SCRAP BOARD

CORNER POST

NOTCHED DECK BOARD

1. Installing the posts.

◆ Determine the length to cut the posts by adding together the width of the deck joists, the thickness of the decking, the desired height of the beams, and 16 inches. Cut four 4-by-4 posts to this length and chamfer the tops *(page 84)*.

◆ Remove deck boards at the edges of the deck, if necessary, to expose the corners of the framing.

◆ From the bottom of a post, measure up the width of the deck joists plus the thickness of the decking and draw a line on the post at this height. Nail a scrap board to the post with its bottom edge on the line.

◆ Set the post in place in the corner, resting the scrap board on top of the decking.

◆ While a helper plumbs the post, drill a hole for a $\frac{3}{8}$- by 5-inch galvanized lag screw through the rim joist into the post and drive the screw partway. Install a second screw through the end joist, then tighten the two screws alternately, keeping the post plumb in both directions *(left)*. Drive a second screw into each side, then remove the scrap board.

◆ Install the remaining posts in the same way.

◆ With a saber saw, notch the deck boards to fit around the posts, then fit the decking in place *(inset)* and nail it down.

2. Bolting the split beams.

◆ On a pair of adjacent posts, mark the desired height of the beams. Extend the mark around each post with a combination square.

◆ Measure the distance between the outer sides of the posts and cut two 2-by-6s 10 inches longer than this distance. Cut off a corner at each end of the pieces *(page 31)*.

◆ Tack a 2-by-6 to each side of the two posts to form a split beam *(page 34)*.

◆ Drill two $\frac{1}{2}$-inch holes through the pair of 2-by-6s and the post, then fasten the boards to the post with $\frac{1}{2}$- by 7-inch carriage bolts *(right)*.

◆ Install the second beam across the opposite pair of posts.

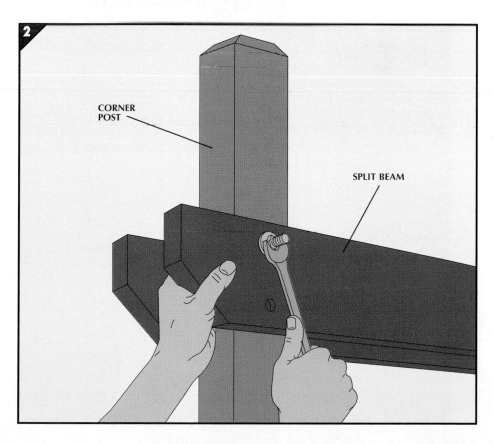

CORNER POST

SPLIT BEAM

3. Adding short posts.

◆ On the beams, mark locations for the short posts that will support the rafters, spacing them evenly between the corner posts and a maximum of 4 feet apart.

◆ Cut a 4-by-4 16 inches long to make each short post, and chamfer one end.

◆ Slip a post between the split beam at a location mark, aligning it flush with the bottom edges of the beam. Plumb the post and fasten it to each 2-by-6 with two $2\frac{1}{2}$-inch coated deck screws *(right)*.

◆ Install the remaining short posts in the same manner.

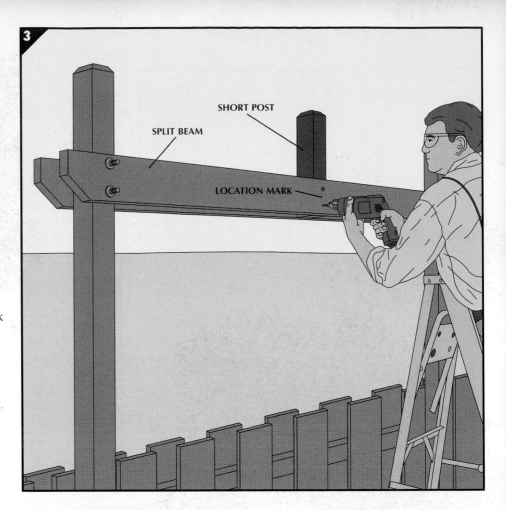

4. Mounting the rafters.

◆ For the split rafters, cut two 2-by-6s long enough to extend past the posts to accommodate two slats of the size and spacing you have chosen. Trim the corners as for the beams.

◆ Set one 2-by-6 across the beams so the overhang is equal at both ends and fasten it to one side of each post with two deck screws.

◆ Attach the second 2-by-6 to the other side of the posts *(left)*.

◆ Fasten the second split rafter over the other beam; then add the intermediate rafters, screwing them to the sides of the short posts.

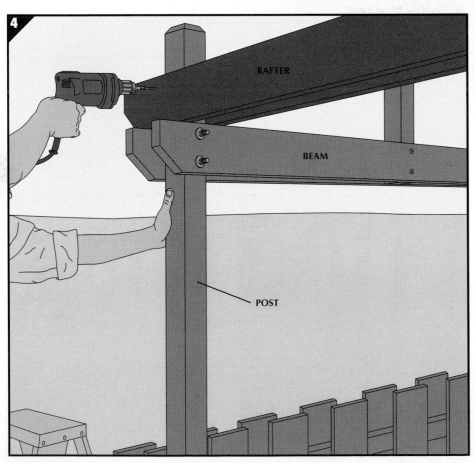

5. Laying the slats.

◆ Cut 2-by-2 slats long enough to overhang the rafters by 2 inches at each end.

◆ Position the first slat across the ends of the rafters and drill pilot holes for $2\frac{1}{2}$-inch coated deck screws where it crosses the rafters; then screw it down. Attach a second slat against the outside faces of the posts and a third slat against their inside faces.

◆ At the opposite end of the rafters, fasten three slats in the same manner.

◆ Following the spacing plan you have determined (page 112), continue adding slats across the rafters, using a spacer made from a scrap board cut to the desired width of the gap between the slats (right).

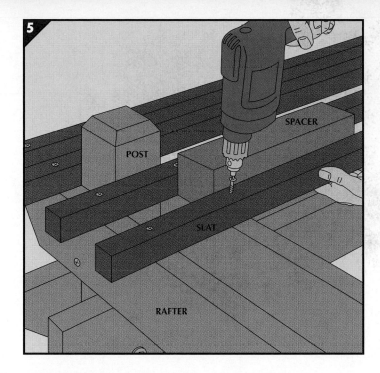

6. Cladding the post bases.

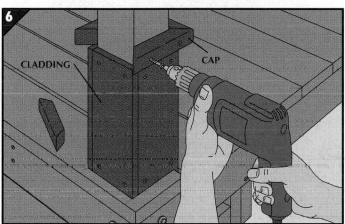

◆ For each corner post, cut four 1-by-6 cladding boards $4\frac{1}{4}$ inches wide and 8 inches long, then fit them around the post at the bottom so each piece overlaps an adjacent one. Fasten the boards to the post with a screw at each corner.

◆ Cut four lengths of 2-by-2 cap pieces to fit around the post, mitering the corners. Resting the caps atop the cladding, fasten each one to the post with two screws (left). Lock each corner with a single screw.

A COVERED CORNER

An overhead need not cover the entire deck—placing it at one corner or end of the deck can shelter that spot while leaving the rest of the deck exposed to sunlight. Track the sun direction at different times of day to help you decide where you most need shade, or place the overhead above a specific feature like a built-in bench or hot tub (right).

Closing in a section of a deck with a high screen instead of a railing offers privacy, shade, and shelter from the wind. It can also serve as a trellis for vines.

Design: A screen's basic structure is similar to that of a railing *(pages 83-93).* Horizontal rails run between 4-by-4 posts notched and fastened to the deck. The space between the rails can be filled in with a variety of materials, including vertical boards or lattice, or a combination of both *(below).* A screen can be virtually any height, but about 6 feet is typical.

Buying Lattice: Lattice for outdoor use comes in cedar, pressure-treated wood, or vinyl and is generally available in 4- by 8- or 2- by 8-foot sheets. The size of the openings in the sheets varies from $1\frac{3}{4}$ inches to $3\frac{5}{8}$ inches—screens with smaller holes provide more privacy. Although you can cut lattice *(page 119, box)* or have it trimmed at the lumberyard, your job will be easier if you can design the screen to incorporate full sheets.

 TOOLS

Circular saw
Electric drill

 **MATERIALS**

Pressure-treated
  1 x 2s, 1 x 6s,
  2 x 2s, 2 x 4s,
  4 x 4s

Lattice ($\frac{1}{2}$")
Deck screws
  (2", $2\frac{1}{2}$")

 SAFETY TIPS

Wear goggles when using a power tool. Put on a dust mask to cut pressure-treated wood, and wash your hands thoroughly after handling the lumber.

Anatomy of a screen.

In the design at right, three rails made of 2-by-4s are attached between 4-by-4 posts, forming upper and lower sections. Posts are set at the ends of the screen and every 8 feet in between. In the bottom section, 2-by-2 cleats run down the middle of the lower and middle rails, and vertical 1-by-6 boards are fastened to the cleats. In this example, successive boards are staggered on each side of the cleats to form a solid barrier when viewed straight on, but they let light through at an angle. The width and spacing of the boards can be varied to achieve the desired effect. The upper section is sized to accommodate a 2- by 8-foot sheet of $\frac{1}{2}$-inch-thick lattice. Vertical 1-by cleats fastened to the posts between the middle and upper rails and horizontal cleats running along the rails hold the lattice in place.

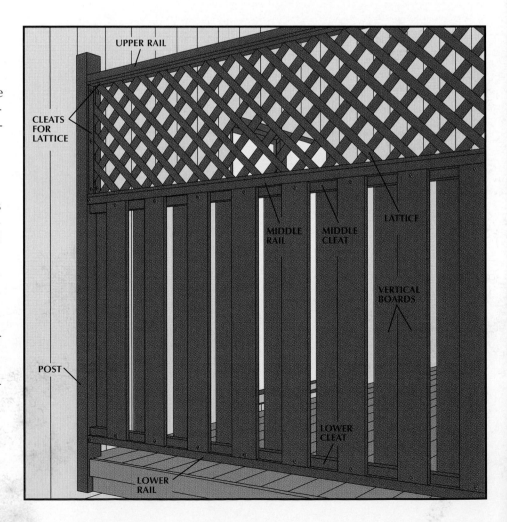

PUTTING UP BOARDS AND LATTICE

MIDDLE RAIL

POST

SPACER

LOWER RAIL

1. Installing posts and rails.

◆ Cut 4-by-4 posts to extend from the bottom of the rim or end joist to the desired height of the screen above the deck. Notch and install a post *(pages 84-86)* at each end of the screen and at least every 8 feet in between.
◆ Cut three 2-by-4s to fit as rails between each pair of adjacent posts.
◆ Set a 2-by-4 spacer on the deck next to each post and place a rail on the spacers.
◆ Fasten the rail to each post, driving a $2\frac{1}{2}$-inch coated deck screw at an angle through the edge of the rail into the post—alternatively, use a galvanized framing anchor.
◆ Mark the height of the middle rail on the posts and, working with a helper, install it in the same way *(left)*.
◆ Mount the upper rail at the desired height.

2. Adding the horizontal cleats.

◆ Cut two 2-by-2 cleats to the same length as the rails.
◆ Center one cleat on the bottom rail and fasten it with a $2\frac{1}{2}$-inch coated deck screw driven every 8 inches *(right)*.
◆ Working with a helper, fasten the second cleat to the underside of the middle rail.

CLEAT

LOWER RAIL

3. Fastening the vertical boards.

◆ Cut 1-by-6 boards to fit between the top and bottom rails, and cut a short spacer from the same stock or from wood that is the width you have chosen for the gaps between boards.

◆ Starting at one end of the screen, butt a 1-by-6 against the post and one side of the upper and lower cleats, then fasten it to the cleats with two 2-inch coated deck screws.

◆ Hold the edge of the spacer against this first board, butt the second board against the spacer, and fasten it to the cleats. Continue to install boards until you reach the opposite post, cutting the last board to width if necessary.

◆ Starting at the same post, install boards on the opposite side of the cleats (*right*), but use the spacer to off-set the first board from the first one on the other side by the width of a board.

SPACER

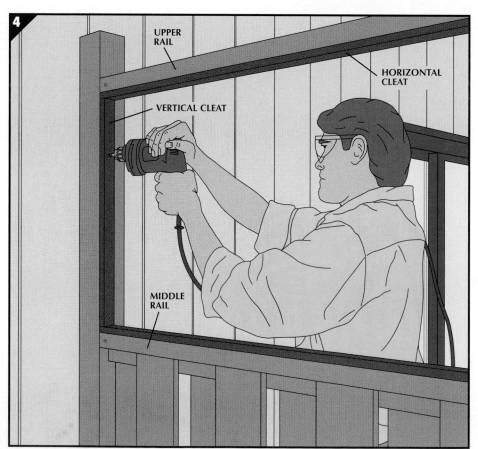

UPPER RAIL

HORIZONTAL CLEAT

VERTICAL CLEAT

MIDDLE RAIL

4. Installing the lattice cleats.

◆ Cut two 1-by-2s to fit between the posts as cleats to support the lattice.

◆ Set a cleat along the middle rail, flush with the outside edge of the screen, and fasten it in place with a deck screw driven every 8 inches.

◆ Attach a cleat to the underside of the upper rail in the same way.

◆ Cut two more cleats to fit vertically between the horizontal cleats. Fasten one to each post flush with the outer edge (*left*).

CLEAT

5. Installing the lattice.
◆ Place the lattice against the cleats and tack it in place.
◆ Install a second set of cleats on the inside of the lattice, butting them tight against the lattice so their edges are flush with the inner edges of the rails and posts *(left)*.

TRICKS OF THE TRADE

Cutting Lattice

Lattice can be tricky to cut because it tends to flex and bind in the saw. For best results, make the cutting mark on the lattice with a chalk line and set the piece on a 2-by-4 on the ground with the cutting mark a few inches past the edge of the board. Check that the lattice is square to the 2-by-4, then tack the lattice to the board in three or four places. Make a cutting jig by attaching a 4-inch strip of particleboard to a 12-inch strip so the factory-cut edge of the narrower piece divides the wider one; then clamp the jig to a work surface. Cut the wider strip with a circular saw, guiding the tool's base plate along the narrower strip. Set

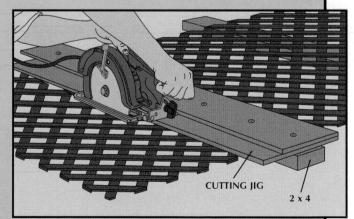

CUTTING JIG

2 x 4

the jig on top of the lattice with the edge aligned with the cutting mark and screw it to the 2-by-4. Install a plywood-cutting blade on the circular saw and cut the lattice, guiding the saw base along the jig *(above)*.

The area under a raised deck can be enclosed with skirting to hide the framing lumber and give the structure a more finished appearance. Skirting also inhibits the growth of weeds beneath the deck because it blocks light. To leave the area accessible for storage, include a door in the design.

Materials: Deck skirts are most often made from lattice panels or vertical boards. Vertical boards are the sturdier choice and provide a more solid support for a door; the style shown below is appropriate for decks up to 4 feet high.

Installation: Board skirting is ideal for a deck with a colonial railing *(pages 88-91)* and either overhanging decking or cap boards between the posts; in this design, the tops of the skirt boards are hidden. A slightly different installation technique is needed for a deck with a traditional railing *(page 122, box).*

 TOOLS

Carpenter's square
Carpenter's level (4')
Chalk line
Circular saw
Electric drill
Screwdriver

 **MATERIALS**

Pressure-treated
  1 x 6s, 2 x 2s, 2 x 4s
Masonry screws ($2\frac{1}{2}$")
Deck screws (2")
Butt hinges (3" x 3")
Gate latch

 SAFETY TIPS

Put on goggles when working with power tools. Add a dust mask when cutting pressure-treated wood; wash thoroughly after handling the lumber.

Anatomy of a board skirt.

In the design shown at right, 1-by-6 boards are fastened to the rim joist under the deck cap *(page 87, box)* or under the decking if it overhangs. Cleats run along the inside of the boards near the bottom, and both the boards and the cleats are pinned together at the corners. Constructed from 1-by-6s with cleats in a Z pattern on the back, the door is hinged to the boards on one side of the opening. A brace attached to the deck framing on each side of the door opening adds stability. For a deck more than 3 feet high, additional braces are installed every 8 feet.

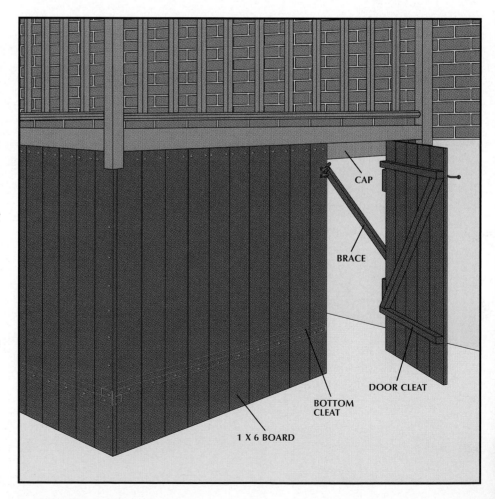

CAP

BRACE

DOOR CLEAT

BOTTOM CLEAT

1 X 6 BOARD

HANGING THE BOARDS

1. Attaching the wall cleat.
◆ With a carpenter's level, mark a plumb line on the house wall in line with the outside face of the end joist.
◆ Cut a 2-by-2 cleat long enough to extend from the bottom of the rim joist to the ground.
◆ While a helper holds the cleat against the house wall flush with the plumb line, drill a pilot hole for a $2\frac{1}{2}$-inch masonry screw through the cleat and into the wall every 8 inches *(left)*, then drive the screws.

2. Fastening the boards.
◆ Measure the distance from the bottom of the cap or overhanging decking to the ground and cut 1-by-6 boards to this length—if the ground is uneven, vary the length of the boards to follow the terrain.
◆ Hold the first board against the wall cleat and outline the bottom of the post on its inner face. Notch the board to fit the post, then fasten it to the end joist with two 2-inch coated deck screws and to the wall cleat with screws driven about every 8 inches.
◆ Set the second board against the first and fasten it to the end joist.
◆ Continue fastening the boards *(right)* until you reach the proposed door opening. Leave a gap $\frac{1}{2}$ inch larger than the combined width of five boards, then resume hanging the boards.
◆ When you are within about 3 feet of the next post, measure the remaining distance and cut the remaining boards to width to fit the space; notch the last board to fit around the post.

SKIRTING A DECK WITH A TRADITIONAL RAILING

A deck with a traditional railing *(pages 91-93)* has no cap or overhanging decking to hide the top of the skirt boards. To hang skirting from this structure, fasten 2-by-6 cleats horizontally along the back of the end and rim joists so about half of each cleat extends past the bottom edge of the joists. You can then attach the skirt boards to the cleats.

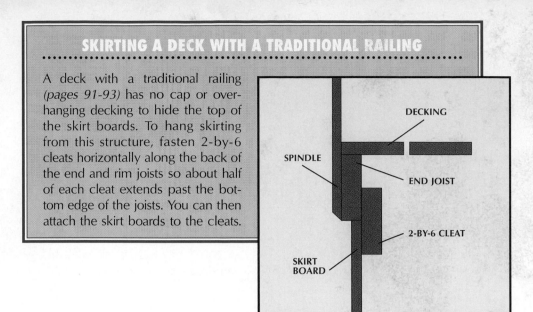

DECKING

SPINDLE

END JOIST

2-BY-6 CLEAT

SKIRT
BOARD

BOTTOM
CLEAT

3. Cleating the boards.

◆ Cut a 2-by-4 cleat to the length of the completed section of skirting. Where there is a door opening, make a cleat for each side of the opening.

◆ On the inside of the skirt, measure down from the top of the end joist and make a mark at each end of the section of skirting about 8 inches above the ground. Measure down the same distance on the outside of the skirt and snap a chalk line along the outer faces of the boards.

◆ Have a helper hold the cleat with its edge against the inside of the skirt, centering it over the mark at each end. Aligning the drill with the chalk line, drive a screw through a skirt board to fasten each end of the cleat *(left)*.

◆ Using the chalk line as a guide, drive a screw through each skirt board into the cleat.

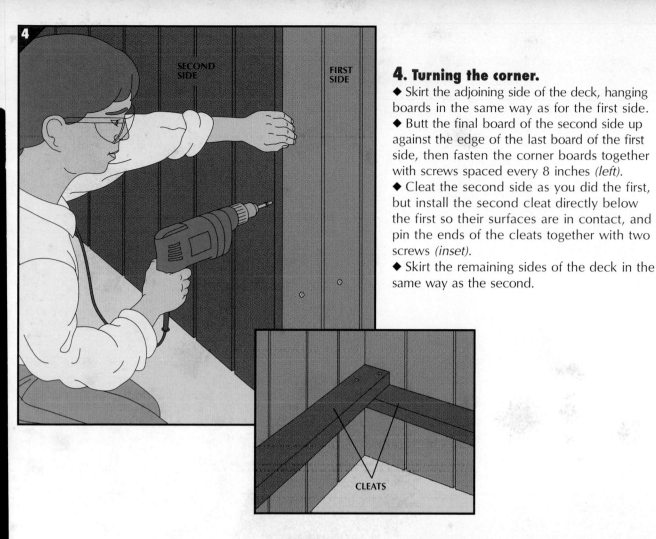

4. Turning the corner.

◆ Skirt the adjoining side of the deck, hanging boards in the same way as for the first side.

◆ Butt the final board of the second side up against the edge of the last board of the first side, then fasten the corner boards together with screws spaced every 8 inches *(left)*.

◆ Cleat the second side as you did the first, but install the second cleat directly below the first so their surfaces are in contact, and pin the ends of the cleats together with two screws *(inset)*.

◆ Skirt the remaining sides of the deck in the same way as the second.

5. Bracing the skirt.

◆ Cut a 2-by-2 6 feet long, mitering one end at 45 degrees.

◆ Rest the mitered end of the brace against a deck joist and the other end against an edge of the door opening.

◆ While a helper plumbs the skirt, mark the brace along the inner face of the skirt board at the opening *(right)*. Miter the brace at the mark.

◆ Use the brace as a template to cut another for the other side of the opening and any additional braces that are required to keep the skirt plumb.

◆ Reposition the first brace between the deck joist and the inside face of the skirting, then fasten it at each end with a deck screw driven at an angle.

◆ Install the remaining braces in the same way.

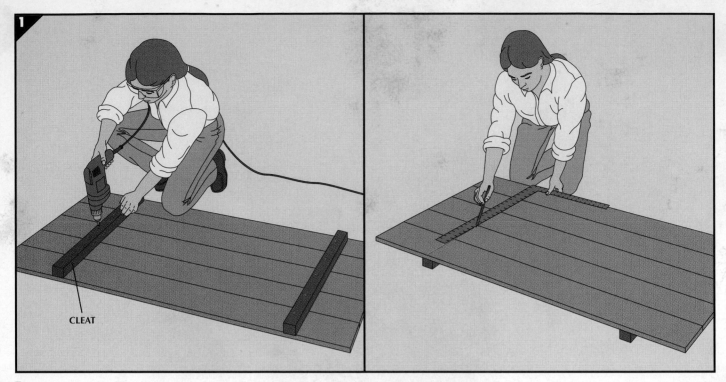

1. Assembling the door.

◆ Cut five boards $\frac{1}{4}$ inch shorter than the skirt boards adjoining the door opening and lay them flat, edge-to-edge and ends aligned.

◆ Make two 2-by-2 cleats to span the width of the boards, place them across the pieces 1 foot from each end, and

attach them to each board with a 2-inch screw *(above, left)*.

◆ Turn the door over and, with a carpenter's square, mark a line across the surface in line with the middle of each cleat *(above, right)*.

◆ Using the line as a guide, drive two screws through each board into the cleat.

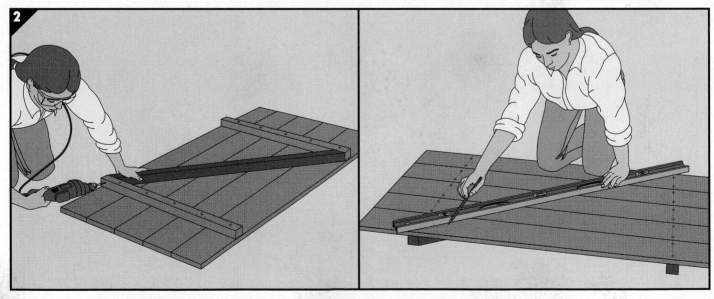

2. Adding a diagonal brace.

◆ Cut a cleat to fit diagonally between the first two as described on page 72, Step 2.

◆ Drive a screw through each horizontal cleat into the end of the diagonal one *(above, left)*.

◆ Turn the door over and, with a straightedge, mark a line across the door in line with the middle of the diagonal cleat *(above, right)*.

◆ Following the line, drive a screw through each board into the diagonal brace.

3. Positioning the door.

◆ Fit the door into its opening $\frac{1}{4}$ inch below the cap or overhanging decking.

◆ While a helper holds the door in position, tack it to the end joist with three screws *(left)*.

4. Hinging the door.

◆ Position a 3- by 3-inch butt hinge about one-quarter of the way down from the top of the door so the pin loops are centered on the seam between the door and the skirt, then mark the screw holes on the door and the adjoining skirt board.

◆ Remove the hinge, drill a pilot hole for a screw at each mark, then fasten the hinge in place *(right)*.

◆ Add a second hinge about one-quarter of the way up from the bottom of the door. For a door more than 3 feet high, add a third hinge between the first two. Remove the three screws installed in Step 3.

◆ Install a gate latch as described on page 95, Step 4.

PIN LOOPS

TIME® LIFE BOOKS

Time-Life Books is a division of Time Life Inc.

TIME LIFE INC.
PRESIDENT and CEO: George Artandi

TIME-LIFE BOOKS
PRESIDENT: Stephen R. Frary
PUBLISHER/MANAGING EDITOR:
Neil Kagan
VICE PRESIDENT, MARKETING:
Steven A. Schwartz

HOME REPAIR AND IMPROVEMENT:
Ultimate Decks
EDITOR: Lee Hassig
DIRECTOR OF MARKETING:
Wells P. Spence
Art Director: Kate McConnell
Text Editor: Karen Sweet
Editorial Assistant: Patricia D. Whiteford

Director of Finance: Christopher Hearing
Directors of Book Production:
Marjann Caldwell, Patricia Pascale
Director of Operations: Betsi McGrath
Director of Photography and Research:
John Conrad Weiser
Director of Editorial Administration:
Barbara Levitt
Production Manager: Marlene Zack
Quality Assurance Manager: James King
Chief Librarian: Louise D. Forstall

ST. REMY MULTIMEDIA INC.
President: Pierre Léveillé
Vice President, Finance: Natalie Watanabe
Managing Editor: Carolyn Jackson
Managing Art Director: Diane Denoncourt
Production Manager: Michelle Turbide

Staff for *Ultimate Decks*

Series Editors: Marc Cassini, Heather Mills
Art Directors: Normand Boudreault,
Robert Paquet
Senior Editor: Brian Parsons
Assistant Editor: Rebecca Smollett
Designers: Jean-Guy Doiron, Robert Labelle
Photographers: Robert Chartier, Martin
Girard, Maryo Proulx
Editorial Assistants: James Piecowye,
Emma Roberts, George Zikos
Coordinator: Dominique Gagné
Indexer: Linda Cardella Cournoyer
Systems Director: Edward Renaud
Technical Support: Jean Sirois
Other Staff: Lorraine Doré, Michel Giguère,
Francine Lemieux

PICTURE CREDITS
Cover: Photograph, Robert Chartier.
Art, Normand Boudreault, Maryo Proulx.

Illustrators: La Bande Créative, Gilles Beauchemin, Frederic F. Bigio from B-C Graphics, Dale Gustafson, Ken Kay, Lennart Johnson Designs, Peter McGinn, Kurt Ortell, Jacques Perrault.

Photographers: **12, 15, 49, 57, 70, 93:** California Redwood Association. **16:** Thermal Industries Inc. **29, 39, 65, 73, 75, 84:** Robert Chartier. **63:** Cepco Tool Co. **80, 115:** Western Red Cedar Lumber Association. **90:** CCD Design/Construction Inc. **97:** Osmose Wood Preserving Company. **107:** Better Built Corporation. **108:** Robert Mowat Associates.

ACKNOWLEDGMENTS
The editors wish to thank the following individuals and institutions: Almost Heaven Ltd., Renick, WV; Archadeck, Richmond, VA; Better Built Corporation, Wilmington, MA; California Redwood Association, Novato, CA; Harvey Carmel, CCD Design/ Construction Inc., Columbia, MD; Cepco Tool Co., Spencer, NY; Club Piscine-Le Supermarché, Brossard, Que.; Ron Conner, Conner's Pool and Spa, San Antonio, TX; Jon Eakes, Montreal, Que.; Hickson Corporation, Smyrna, GA; Maxx Inc., Sainte-Marie, Que.; Robert Mowat Associates, San Francisco, CA; Osmose Wood Preserving Inc., Griffin, GA; Pacific Group International, Walnut Creek, CA; Simpson Strong-Tie Company Inc., Pleasanton, CA; Southern Forest Products Association, Kenner, LA; Joe Teets, Centerville, VA; Thermal Industries Inc., Pittsburgh, PA; Trex Company, Winchester, VA; Western Red Cedar Lumber Association, Vancouver, BC; Joseph Wood, Wood's Shop Creative Builders, Spring Valley, CA; World Floor Covering Association, Anaheim, CA.

**Library of Congress
Cataloging-in-Publication Data**
Ultimate decks / by the editors of Time-Life
  Books.
  p. cm. — (Home repair and improvement)
Includes index.
ISBN 0-7835-3923-1
1. Decks (Architecture, Domestic)—Design
  and construction—Amateurs' manuals.
I. Time-Life Books. II. Series.
TH4970.U48   1998
690'.893—dc21   98-4263
                                        CIP